leader.

The
Buzz

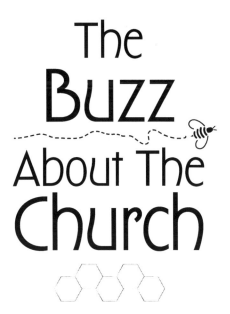

About The
Church

Re-Imagining Discipleship
Through the Metaphor
of Beekeeping

MATTHEW THOMAS

WESTBOW
PRESS®
A DIVISION OF THOMAS NELSON
& ZONDERVAN

WestBow Press books may be ordered through booksellers or by contacting:

WestBow Press
A Division of Thomas Nelson & Zondervan
1663 Liberty Drive
Bloomington, IN 47403
www.westbowpress.com
1 (866) 928-1240

ISBN: 978-1-5127-9352-9 (sc)
ISBN: 978-1-5127-9351-2 (hc)
ISBN: 978-1-5127-9353-6 (e)

Library of Congress Control Number: 2017909981

Print information available on the last page.

WestBow Press rev. date: 7/5/2017

Contents

Acknowledgments

This project was born several years ago with a call to write. God has always communicated with me by whispering words joined with an unbelievable persistence. Somewhere in the back of my mind, I knew I was supposed to write about theology and honeybees. The idea of creating a theology of beekeeping and marrying it to discipleship was born many years later in the lobby of a Seattle hotel with a doctoral cohort I have come to regard as dear friends.

Thank you, my dear friends, Douglas Witherup, Norbert Haukenfrers, Tim Wilson, Danny Russell, Rick Callahan, Patrick Sehl, Paula Jones, Rob Parker, Bryce Ashlin-Mayo, Scott Ness, Shane Sebastian, Kevin Glenn, Greg Borror, and Len Calhoun. Love you guys!

To the faculty and staff of George Fox Evangelical Seminary, thank you for helping me to dig deep and for guiding me along this journey of discovery. Thank you for making me better, Loren Kerns and Clifford Berger. I am grateful for you!

Another major contributor to the final product has been my editor, Judy Hagey. Thank you for your way with words. This project would have never come to fruition if weren't for my academic advisor, Phil Carnes. Thank you for pushing and pulling me to *bee* better.

Several years ago, I received the opportunity and privilege of a lifetime when I was accepted into the doctoral program at George Fox Seminary. It has been a joy and adventure studying with you, Leonard Sweet. Thank you for discipling me and calling me "friend." God is good at putting mentors in front of us and vice versa.

When I was sixteen years old, my grandfather began to disciple me in the art of beekeeping. Most of what I know about honeybees and how to steward them came at his feet. I never imagined those experiences with my grandfather would translate into my own personal love for beekeeping and then merge the ideas I learned there with disciple making. I would also like to thank the other important beekeeper of my life, Art Thomas, my father.

To my parents, siblings, and dear friends, I thank you! A special acknowledgment and thanks to Whitehouse United Methodist Church for your love and support through this process. The ideas found in these pages took shape and found expression in your presence. For the people who have sacrificed the most, I dedicate this book to you! For my dear wife, Christina, and my kids, Noah and Emma, I love you very much.

To my friend Tommy Rosenblad, thanks for inviting me out on that Sager Street balcony.

Introduction

The rapid decline of the North American church has many concerned. Since the beginning of the twentieth century, membership in the North American church has fallen drastically. Losses in membership and attendance have created a "buzz about the church." According to findings by George Barna, the unchurched population has increased from 24 to 34 percent in one decade.[1] In *Pilgrim Practices: Discipleship for a Missional Church*, Kristopher Norris tells us, "For years pastors, pollsters, and academics have been signaling the death of the church, or at least the death of the church as we know it. Church attendance in most North American denominations is plummeting."[2]

There have been many attempts to identify the root problem or cause of the decline. Some, like Barbara Brown Taylor, suggest overintellectualization of the faith. Others clamor over influences like the Enlightenment, Gnosticism, and fundamentalism as roots and symptoms alike. Some identify the problem as the Christian faith being no longer relevant or intelligible in its current thought forms to the modern culture. Regardless, a 2001 survey reported in the *Christian Science Monitor* reveals that the number of Americans who have "'no religious preference' has doubled from 1990 to 2001, reaching 14 percent of the population."[3]

---

[1] George Barna, *The State of the Church 2002* (Ventura, CA: Issachar Resources, 2002), 17..

[2] Kristopher Norris, *Pilgrim Practices: Discipleship for a Missional Church* (Eugene, OR: Cascade Books, 2012), Kindle Location 140..

[3] Reggie McNeal, *The Present Future: Six Tough Questions for the Church* (San Francisco: Jossey-Bass, 2003), Kindle Location 277.

Institutional tendencies of the modern church and me-centered, gimmick-type churches, on the other extreme, are equally concerning. Many affirm the church has become the mirrored image of the consumeristic culture, offering flash but very little substance. In addition to diagnosing the problem, many have offered numerous solutions. Recovering a missional flavor, enhancing worship and program experiences, leaving the mainline church, or recovering a Jesus approach to discipleship, to name a few, are all responses to a declining church. Questions like why people have left the church and why others aren't signing up consume our time and energy. Other questions like "Can the North American church recover and become a viable carrier of the gospel again?" equally consume our attention.

Beyond the relevancy issue the church faces, it also must grapple with whether or not the theology, doctrine, and practices of mainline and evangelical traditions, in past and recent history, are adequate to sustain the future church. Are our ancient doctrinal positions and hermeneutical stances partly responsible for the shape of modern Christianity? Undoubtedly yes! In our pursuit to defend the faith since Martin Luther, have we missed something in our spiritual pilgrimage that has the potential to renew the face of the world and church? The title of Leonard Sweet's book, *What Matters Most: How We Got the Point But Missed the Person*, suggests the enormity of the loss. We found orthodoxy but lost Jesus.

I am arguing the above diagnosis for the church's decline and the subsequent symptoms are correct, but I would add the church is failing or in decline because it hasn't handed over a comprehensive Christian faith. While content is of significant value, a delivery system is equally important. Many focus on the message of Jesus and ignore his divine method. What has been passed on is a spiritually unsustainable religion. *The Buzz about the Church: Reimagining Discipleship through the Metaphor of Beekeeping* fosters conversation and offers a solution to decline by studying God's honeybees and Jesus's methodology of discipleship together.

Modern theology and practice tips its hat to acknowledge a truly transcendent God and marvelous creation. However, the Lord has given us more than just a beautiful creation to admire and protect.

Simply posturing with scathing acknowledgment has left our theologies emaciated. Creation, as the spoken and, by extension, living Word of God, has been often overlooked or marginally recognized to the detriment of faith development. In the Genesis account, God's creation was spoken into existence and subsequently is living. The question that comes to the front when the church has spent considerable time, energy, and attention wrestling with theological positioning and spiritual correctness is what has been sacrificed. One of the answers to that question is the divine revelation of creation.

In the beginning chapters of the book of Genesis, God spoke the world into existence. *Ex nihilo* (out of nothing) God spoke, and life began. The living God created living things by utterance. His first command to all creation was to do what he had done in creation, namely "be fruitful and multiply and fill the earth" (Gn 1:28). The Creator gave his creation the means by which to multiply and reproduce. The seed, egg, and rib were the great gifts of creation. Continuation of life would not be possible without any of these three plus one more, pollination. The process of pollination makes the circle of life continue. Growth and reproductive maturity are the fruit of pollination. The good news is God gave all creation the opportunity to participate in his creative process. Creation truly is an authoritative testament to the divine disclosure. We see God's playfulness and wisdom in what he has made. Creation is the cradle of life, a new testament to the power, authority, processes, and love of God.

Creation teaches us about God and the processes that serve to mature our faith, for within creation is the process of maturity we call discipleship. Likewise the very process and fundamental ideas of creation are mirrored in the life and ministry of Jesus, which you will discover. It makes sense though. The God who created the material world showed up through the process he had made. If we carefully look at the life of Jesus and his methodology for maturing his followers, we will also begin to see the same process Jesus used was the one utilized when he created the world *ex nihilo* and the one he continues to use to bring maturity to life.

Jesus called twelve disciples and did life with them. They began the process en route to maturity and spiritual reproduction. Jesus would invest his life, teach them about his ways and kingdom, set an example in word and action, and love them in deep and abiding relationship. Jesus modeled obedience and grace, process, and relationship. I believe Jesus was the greatest disciple maker of all time. Not only did he share the life-giving message for the world he created, he also provided the vehicle for passing that message to the next generation. From a very small nucleus of untrained people, the Great Beekeeper fashioned them to carry on his message through a delivery system. Jesus didn't just leave us content for our nourishment; he left us a methodology to bring followers to maturity.

From the heart of creation comes a metaphor that reveals the divine process of maturing followers. We will raise the lid on a hive of honeybees to more deeply understand and experience the process of making disciples. You will be amazed at what you will discover about God and the connection from exploring a beehive. Of all the great metaphors available for telling the story of God's divine disclosure, honeybees fly to the top of the list. As you will see, the life of a colony of honeybees offers us every virtue and process through a highly advanced community on mission, which has often been termed "communitas."

What is recovered here is the methodology of discipleship Jesus modeled through the lens of beekeeping. However, this offering isn't just another mechanical approach to discipleship where I lay out the strategies or nuts and bolts approach. Rather, it is an approach that marries Jesus's template with beekeeping. The goal is for the church to recover and hand over the Christian faith to the next generation of followers. What is handed over isn't just the preexistent content of orthodoxy. The new metaphor of beekeeping passes on a more robust and comprehensive view of Christianity. It is a new lens in which to view Jesus's ministry. As a result, it is hoped the reader will have a deeper knowledge of and relationship with the God who made it all, redeems it all, and loves it all.

For the past several years, there has been a much-needed resurgence in the subject of discipleship. No doubt, one of the reasons for this rally is due to the decline of the North American church. As a result, numerous books and articles have been written to address the return of the lost art of disciple making. This book is a contribution to the current conversation on how to make followers of Jesus Christ. It is both a theoretical and practical contribution with a twist. Since I am marrying metaphor with theology, it is important to communicate to you how and why I am undertaking this marriage.

Why beekeeping? Let me tell you the story of the how and why. The Christian life is a semiotic journey of discovering the fullness of the living God. On this journey, we discover who God really is and who we are in relationship with him. On the road, the signs of his activity are illuminated. The discovery will take introspection and hopefully lead to fruitfulness. Here then is my story.

Several years ago, I was attending a camp at my conference's retreat center outside of Palestine, Texas. I remember the day very well because it was storming and one of my colleagues and I were visiting outside under the portico. He mentioned this doctor of ministry program he was currently a part of. We finished our conversation and went our separate ways.

A year later, that conversation with my friend came to the front of my memory. I went to the computer and began to research the program. The program is through George Fox Evangelical Seminary, and the degree is in semiotics and future studies. I had never heard the word "semiotics" before. Its basic meaning is the study of signs. Crystal Downing once claimed, to understand the culture, "responsible Christians must become skilled sign-readers, able to distinguish among diverse cultural powers in order to access their threat and respond appropriately."[4]

This book, in part, is an attempt to articulate the signs of God's activity in creation. Jesus was the chief semiotician. The first disciples Jesus made were semioticians. Jesus taught his disciples how to read the signs. Modern disciples are taught to read the signs of God's activity among us.

After being spurred to enter the program, I signed up. The journey of a lifetime began and set this Christian on a course that would change my life. In this highly relational cohort-based program with a leading mentor, we set sail. The first year we met in Portland, Oregon, and the second year we met in Seattle, Washington. In this second encounter

---

[4] Crystal L. Downing, *Changing Signs of Truth: A Christian Introduction to the Semiotics of Communication* (Downers Grove, IL: IVP Academic, 2012), Kindle Location 128..

with the other members of the cohort and my mentor, God called me to a holy marriage.

In this group of seventeen, we split up into groups of four to talk about our projects. Each of us brought to the table an abstract of what we wanted to write about. In my group were Rob, Norbert, and Doug. Everybody in the group shared their thoughts on everyone else's abstract. I was last to get feedback.

My friend Doug was sitting directly across from me. He looked up and said, "Matt, I'm bored."

When he first said it, I was somewhat offended. Then he explained what he meant. It wasn't what I wrote. It was the subject. The topic of discipleship has been on the modern church radar for the past several years and is a bit frayed. Everybody is tired of hearing about discipleship or spiritual formation.

He finished his comments by saying, "Matt, if you used beekeeping to talk about discipleship, I would buy that because it is interesting."[5]

Just as soon as it came out of his mouth, I realized God was speaking. It was a God moment, a true semiotic experience. This is the reason you have a book before you that ceremonially marries discipleship and beekeeping.

While this is interesting, it is only a part of the adventure. The rest of the semiotic story is when I realized all of my life has been preparation for writing a theological book on beekeeping. The calling to write this was as strong and clear as my calling to the ordained ministry. For years, God has been nudging me to write about honeybees and ministry. I asked God to tell me what and expected him to open up my head and dump a revelation over my brain.

A little voice whispered to me, "Do the work."

It wasn't going to be a seamless flow of information, but rather writing that was born from deep-seated trials and pains in the brain. Beekeeping and discipleship are a metaphorical marriage. The holy union has produced a new way of understanding the call of the Lord to make followers.

---

[5] Personal conversation with Doug Witherup and other members of the doctoral cohort in the lobby of hotel in downtown Seattle. May 2011.

It was only recently that a holy marriage occurred between beekeeping and discipleship. My family has been keeping bees for many decades, so honeybees have always been on the interest radar. I'm a fourth-generation apiarist and learned how to keep bees from my grandfather, Cliff Thomas. My grandfather and great-grandfather learned from another of my great-grandfathers, Arthur Banta (1896–1989), who got interested in bees while attending the University of California at Davis. Beekeeping, like disciple making, is something that is passed on to the next generations.

Like beekeeping, discipleship has always held a special place in this follower's heart. In my twenty-year pastorate, one of the most frustrating aspects is the level of maturity that is found in the church. Disciple making, as Jesus modeled it, is mostly absent from the parish, and it shows. There are signs, however, of disciple making but in limited ministry contexts.

Who would have ever bridged disciple making with beekeeping? Only the Creator would have a revelation which could unravel his church and create such a buzz his people would have to take notice! The bridge has always been there but has been hidden from our sight. I can envision a bridge hidden by briars and snares that the thick foliage has completely canvased. This less-traveled bridge of nature, metaphor, and story has eluded many Christians, but as I share in the book, it holds something of value for all who decide to follow Jesus Christ. What we will discover when we lift the lid on the beehive is a new world and robust discipleship.

When I began the process of research and writing, my goal was to write a book restrictively on disciple making the way Jesus modeled it. What I didn't realize when I nodded to God was this project was going to have a broader theological scope, and the marriage between the process of discipleship and the metaphor of beekeeping would be difficult to reunite. The Christian world is steeped in theological gridlock and centuries of embedded theological rightness. This alone is deterrent enough in wanting to produce a new theology and grand perspective. The language of the modern church is inherited, along with theologies, histories, and stuckness. These are the briars before mentioned. The total history and theology of the church isn't completely riddled with shortsightedness and stuckness. Simply they offer challenge with producing new perspectives for an established church. I suspect, when you make a claim that discipleship can be reimagined through a metaphor of beekeeping, you will likely have pushback and have to do new and groundbreaking theological work. This was the case for me. My hope is you will discover and be inspired as we reimagine discipleship in the most unlikely place. I would also hope that this book brings an awareness and love for God's creation in general and honeybees specifically.

A few more words of introduction are needed. Let me introduce my metaphor with another metaphor. Discipleship is the engine that engages the vehicle (church). Without the engine, the vehicle will be abandoned for other modes of transportation. If the church doesn't have an engine, it's going to be really difficult to fulfill our commission to make followers. If the church is the vehicle, discipleship is the engine, and our destination is maturity and reproduction, then what is missing? The answer is metaphor. Discipleship has long needed a metaphor to create highways, open pathways, and close damaged roads. Metaphors clear the bridge of the briars and thorns. If our goal is to help the church make followers who then make followers, discipleship will need to grab hold of a sound metaphor to help us along our way. Beekeeping is a metaphor that will enable us to see discipleship in fresh and renewed dimensions.

Jesus was a master at metaphor. He was such a master that you and I can easily call to memory his story. His life and message was tied closely to metaphor. In a similar demonstration, we are interweaving the process of discipleship Jesus modeled with a metaphor out of creation. By the end of this book, you won't be able to forget the connections made here. And for you teachers and preachers of the Christian faith, this book provides you reservoirs of pulpit and classroom material. Hopefully you will wrestle with the idea that there is more theologically and naturally than what most of what us preachers contend over, like the questions arising out of Calvinism and Armenianism.

Jesus is a beekeeper, and we are his hive. Now that you have been hooked, let's give our metaphor a hook. Let's begin in an unusual way that will light our way! Let's begin with a riddle.

"Tell us your riddle," they said. "Let's hear it."

He replied, "Out of the eater, something to eat; out of the strong, something sweet." (Jgs 14:13–14 NIV)

Samson told this riddle, but his audience didn't get it. Granted, it was a tough one. It is as tough as our dilemma of church decline. The answer to the riddle is the substance of this book. The recovery of the lost art of discipleship has been reimagined through a metaphor of beekeeping. Like Samson, the carcass of the lion might just have something sweet for us to reach in and grab. Journey with me across the hidden bridge to answer the riddle of what is strong and sweet.

Matthew Thomas
Between South Fork and Durango, Colorado
July 12, 2016

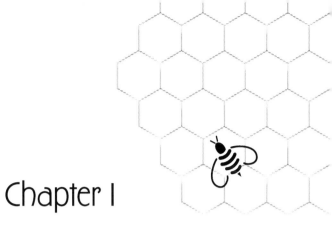

Chapter 1

Church Collapse Disorder (CCD): Lifting the Lid

In the honeybee world, the apiarists (beekeepers) don't really know what is going on inside the colony until they crack the lid. They might expect issues just by observing the entrance of the hive since the entrance of the hive reveals the strength of the colony but doesn't tell the story of its future. Only when the lid is cracked open does the beekeeper detect the true story. The distinct sound of buzzing wings is a beautiful sound. Deeper still, a true testament to the future vitality of the colony is only revealed when frames of brood and honey are pulled out of the bee box. While a hive can look healthy from the outside and even have the appearance of strength when the lid is removed, pests or disease may be lurking upon closer inspection.

Honeybees glue down their lids, so at a certain time of the year, the lids make a very distinct sound when you pry them open with a hive tool. Before taking your hive tool and cracking open the lid, it is best to give the entrance of the hive a couple puffs of smoke from the smoker. The smoke makes the bees think their hive is on fire, so they immediately start consuming honey. When they do, it makes them lethargic, like you and me when we eat too much. Smoking the colony helps manage aggressive bees.

Under the lid lies a world many have never seen. It is where the beekeeper will discover the health of a colony. Just beneath the lid lies the reality of what is and what will come. You can't really tell the health of a beehive until you investigate. Like a beehive, the church needs its lid lifted. It is hard to know the health of a church until we investigate the nest or its nursery. The nursery tells the tale of its future.

One of the smells that permeates the colony and rushes out when the lid is lifted is the sweet smell of honey. Just under the lid are stores of honey or empty frames of wax. The smell we don't want to smell when we crack the top is death, which has a very distinct smell, like something rotting.

Most of us have heard about the drastic losses in honey bee colonies across the United States. Many entomologists and beekeepers alike believe the reason for drastic losses in colonies is due to a condition called "colony collapse disorder." These losses are stemmed by stresses on the bees caused by predators and various pesticides that infect the pollen the bees collect and eat. Many researchers identify the symptoms of colony collapse disorder. They write,

> The winter of 2006/2007 witnessed large-scale losses of managed honey bee (*Apis melliferaL.*) colonies in the United States. Those losses continued into the winter of 2007/2008. In the U.S., a portion of the dead and dying colonies were characterized *post hoc* by a common set of specific symptoms: (1) the rapid loss of adult worker bees from affected colonies as evidenced by weak or dead colonies with excess brood populations relative to adult bee population; (2) a noticeable lack of dead worker bees both within and surrounding the affected hives; and (3) the delayed invasion of hive pests (e.g., small hive beetles and wax moths) and kleptoparasitism from neighboring honey bee colonies [3]. Subsequently, this syndrome has been termed Colony Collapse Disorder, or CCD.[6]

Bees are stressed beyond their limits because of natural predators, diseases, migration, and poisons. Beekeepers return to their colonies and find them collapsed or collapsing. Although honeybee populations and

---

[6] Dennis vanEngelsdorp et al., "Colony Collapse Disorder: A Descriptive Study," *PLOS ONE* 4, no. 8 (2009): e6481, doi:10.1371/journal.pone.0006481.

honey production have been in decline for years, only recently has the condition been diagnosed as colony collapse disorder (CCD). The loss to beekeeping businesses, farmers, and ranchers has been devastating. While much of the disorder remains a mystery, strong indicators point to toxins as the ultimate killer. Several researchers observed that the loss of honeybee populations through CCD "involves an interaction between pathogens and other stress factors."[7] Colonies weakened by pathogens and stress factors experience a rise of *kleptoparasitism*, "an animal that steals food or prey from another animal."[8]

The church in North America has experienced similar catastrophic losses and influence. These losses have contributed to kleptoparasitism in churches. Like honeybee colonies, our churches have experienced collapse due to cultural stresses, spiritual toxins, and changes. Throughout this book, this condition will be referred to as church collapse disorder. This disorder has created quite a buzz among clergy and laity!

Colony Collapse Disorder breaks down the highly structured social dimensions of a hive and keeps the colony from its mission of foraging for food and raising its young. The end result is an unstable and collapsing nursery. Likewise, church collapse disorder keeps us from fulfilling our mission to hand over our faith to the next generations. Dr. William Abraham, Albert Outler Professor for Wesley Studies at Perkins School of Theology, notes this collapse and observes that what the decline of Protestantism "brings home to him is the crucial inability to hand over the faith from one generation to the next."[9]

Professors Kenda Creasy Dean, William Abraham, Leonard Sweet, the late C. S. Lewis, and a host of other scholars identify this as the pivotal issue for the church: passing on the Christian faith to the next

---

[7] Ibid.

[8] "Kleptoparasite," Amateur Entomologists Society, accessed October 1, 2014, http://www.amentsoc.org/insects/glossary/terms/kleptoparasite.

[9] "Billy Abraham on Engaging the Culture," accessed August 12, 2013, http://johnmeunier.wordpress.com/tag/william-j-abraham.

generation.[10] They suggest the church has lost its way, and at the heart of the matter, they claim it has developed somewhat of an identity crisis. If they are correct, then the church will no doubt need to recover its identity, its heritage, and a vehicle by which to pass on the faith. The problem addressed here is the failure of the church to transmit the faith because it is collapsing on itself.

Just under the lid of a hive suffering from CCD is a decaying and declining colony, the smell of which is hard to stomach. The church is struggling to redefine itself in the postmodern world. It lacks theological clarity, is strained by hermeneutical approaches, and has lost the art of making followers. As a result, the sacred faith has not been handed over to the next generations, and the church is steadily shrinking and becoming irrelevant to the culture.

Two main issues rise to the surface:

1. The theological health of the modern church with its strained and often unsatisfying hermeneutical approaches
2. The diminished practice of disciple making

When investigating the health of a colony, the first place you go is the brood nest, which will reveal the issues facing the colony and tell the real story about the colony's future. The brood nest of the church is its nursery and reveals problems in maturing and graduating disciples of Jesus.

A peek under the lid of the church also reveals a colony that is collapsing. We have experienced staggering losses in the mainline and evangelical wings of the church. Upon inspection of the brood nest,

---

[10] The inclusion of these prominent theologians is meant to give weight to the argument. Kenda Creasy Dean has authored a book entitled *Almost Christian*, and in this book, she shares her discovery that modern teenagers are being handed a religion called *moralistic therapeutic deism*. William Abraham is the Albert Outler Chair of Wesley Studies at Perkins School of Theology and has lectured and written extensively on the transmission of the faith. Leonard Sweet is also a United Methodist Scholar and has authored numerous books dealing with transmission of the faith. C. S. Lewis published numerous essays, one of which is "The Transmission of Christianity." Lewis's essay can be found in the book *God in the Dock*.

we have discovered the social or relational makeup of the colony has disintegrated in addition to incarnational failure. These churches are marked by fewer followers and have no clear-cut process for making disciples. They are sick. The smell permeating the modern church comes from our vacant nursery. Church collapse disorder is a very real and serious condition of the North American church.

Diseases and pests that burrow their way into the life of a colony are slow starters and strong finishers. Certain diseases like foul brood or pests like the Varroa mite can wreak havoc on a colony if not inspected and treated early. Both diseases and mites affect honeybee populations and are debilitating in nature. Mites transmit viral loads to the bees, which makes the superorganism sick and weak. With losses in bee population, a hive's social order is disturbed. This disruption keeps the hive agitated and in decline until it collapses on itself. If undiagnosed and left untreated, the chance for colony survival is minimal. The key to strong hives is regular checks for disruptions. "Investigate, investigate, and investigate" is the mantra of beekeeping.

The lid of the modern-day church has also been removed. What has been discovered is, in fact, that the church is collapsing on itself. The problem of the modern-day church not transmitting the faith to the next generation or sharing an alternative faith is essentially a brood-rearing problem. Some predators and diseases have infected our processes for maturing disciples for Jesus Christ. As a result, our social order or faith-forming relationships and communities have been disrupted. One of the most profound and deadly predators on the church's vitality, and I will speak more to it later, is the culture of consumerism.

Based on a December 2010 Barna Group survey, six major themes emerged to give evidence to nontransmission of the Christian faith. Three of the themes outlined by the Barna Group that are important for this research were the following, "The Christian church is becoming less theologically literate, Christians are becoming more ingrown and less outreach-oriented, and the influence of Christianity on culture and individual lives is largely invisible."[11]

---

[11] Barna Group, "2010," accessed September 5, 2014, https://www.barna.org/culture-articles/462-six-megathemes-emerge-from-2010.

Researcher Thom Rainer supports Barna Group's finding with his own and suggests "the number one reason for the decline in church attendance is that members attend with less frequency than they did just a few years ago."[12] Reduced frequency in attendance will contribute to biblical and theological illiteracy, fewer operational and missional resources, and reduced missional presence. "A new study by the Barna Group conducted among 16- to 29-year-olds shows that a new generation is more sceptical of and resistant to Christianity than were people of the same age just a decade ago."[13]

In the same study, Barna revealed "common negative perceptions include that present-day Christianity is judgmental (87%), hypocritical (85%), old-fashioned (78%), and too involved in politics (75%)—representing large proportions of young outsiders who attach these negative labels to Christians."[14]

Scholar and historian Leonard Sweet also observes deficits and unhealthiness in the modern church. Sweet claims, "We are likely the last generation to be familiar with the Christian story and for whom churches have cultural significance. And you will die, leaving behind a culture for whom the Christian story will be completely unknown."[15] Whether Sweet's prophesy will come to pass is, of course, yet to be determined. What is clear, according to Sweet, is the church's impact and significance in the culture is deteriorating. In many respects, the Christian story is lost from our culture and many of our churches.

John Wesley, founder of the eighteenth-century Methodist movement, observed about his church what we observe about ours. He once noted,

---

[12] Thom S. Rainer, "The Number One Reason for the Decline in Church Attendance and Five Ways to Address It," accessed September 5, 2014, http://thomrainer.com/2013/08/19/the-number-one-reason-for-the-decline-in-church-attendance-and-five-ways-to-address-it.

[13] Barna Millenials, "A New Generation Expresses its Skepticism and Frustration with Christianity," accessed September 15, 2014, https://www.barna.org/barna-update/millennials/94-a-new-generation-expresses-its-skepticism-and-frustration-with-christianity#.VBMhHT-YbIU.

[14] Barna Millenials.

[15] Leonard Sweet, *So Beautiful: Divine Design for Life and the Church* (Colorado Springs: David C. Cook Publishers, 2009), Kindle Location 238.

> I am not afraid that the people called Methodist should ever cease to exist either in Europe or America. But I am afraid lest they should only exist as a dead sect, having the form of religion without the power. And this undoubtedly will be the case unless they hold fast to the doctrine, spirit, and discipline with which they first set out.[16]

Wesley, an Anglican priest in the Church of England, saw firsthand that a church that loses its "doctrine, spirit and discipline"[17] dies. He feared they would end up like the Church of England, having religion without the power. It was always Wesley's intention to renew the Church of England. Unfortunately his hope didn't come to pass. Instead a movement emerged that eventually formed the Methodist Episcopal Church in Baltimore, Maryland, in 1784.

Some of the predators of the modern-day church that undermine our mission and community orientation ultimately affect our ability to mature followers of Jesus are many. The cultural insistence on individualism over community, effects of consumerism's ideology, and the breakdown of family dynamics are a few of the cultural paradigm shifts the modern church has to contend with. When the culture and church are at odds concerning the value of each of the above, the result is a disparity in the same. Perhaps the most powerful threat to the church, discipleship, and the culture by and large is consumerism.

Born out of Enlightenment ideals, consumerism became the "mediator of value."[18] Any assessment or diagnosis of current realities of both church and culture will have to take this influence into consideration. If Luther's rebellion leads ultimately to the Enlightenment period and out of that period capitalism is born, one could say then inadvertently that the Protestant Reformation is responsible for consumerism. Alan Hirsch, missional community spokesperson and former advertiser points out, as modern church members,

---

[16] John Wesley, "Thoughts Upon Methodism," in *The Form and Power of Religion: John Wesley on Methodist Vitality* (Eugene, OR: Cascade Books, 2012), 1.
[17] Ibid.
[18] Hirsch, *The Forgotten Ways*, Kindle location 1387.

We have been profoundly discipled every day by a very sophisticated system called media and advertisement. The goal of which is to create desire. Anyone who comes to Jesus in a Western context is already a well discipled consumer, and it is a religion! Consumerism is defined by what we consume. It is the search for meaning, identity, purpose, and belonging tied to the consumption of products. Consumerism is the alternative religion of our day. You can't build a church on consumerism. They will desert you at a moment's notice because they have no commitments beyond their own needs.[19]

The goal of media and advertisement is to create desire so people will consume products in the hope that consumption will bring them meaning, clarify their identities, fill them with purpose, and give them connection or belonging. Vincent Beresford notes,

Consumerism has saturated and centered itself in our culture in the United States. Consumerism now shapes how we think about everything, including religion. Consumers feel "entitled" to have options, getting exactly what they want, and have become consumed with immediate gratification.[20]

Consequently consumerism has done more to rob people of meaning, purpose, identity, and belonging. Catherine Wallace observes,

The problem is a rootless society structurally dependent in a variety of ways upon ever-escalating levels of material acquisition at the expense of human happiness, community, and moral significance. The authors adeptly and repeatedly acknowledge that various religious

---

[19] Alan Hirsch, "Disciple-Making," (Verge Conference, Austin, TX, 2010), accessed February 2012, www.youtube.com/watch?v=NN3oA5AETuI.

[20] Vincent Beresford, *Becoming Fully Human: Re-Imagining Christian Discipleship for an Emerging Generation* (DMin diss., George Fox Evangelical Seminary, 2010), 183.

traditions warn against what has become the American way of life.[21]

Wendy Tremayne, creator of Swap-O-Rama-Rama, says,

> There is no creativity in consumerism. Branding is a huge part of our culture and divides humanity into socio-economic stalls. The consumer is largely asked to express their uniqueness by being selectors. Makers don't make good consumers. The less you know, the less you make, the more you buy.[22]

Creativity, according to Tremayne, is stifled by consumption. Instead of creating, we simply become selectors of goods and services. "A loss of creativity is a loss of imagination. For creativity has its source in imagination."[23]

Visitors who come to the church on Sunday are usually selectors. They are shopping for meaning, purpose, identity, and connection. We give them exactly what they desire—from relevant worship styles to bells-and-whistles programs. In response to the market demand and fear of declining numbers, the church has adopted a seeker-sensitive/attractional model.

Under this model, the church views persons as "market shares."[24] Such an approach also ignites a competition between most churches.[25] In the attractional model, the catchphrase is "come and see." The selectors

---

[21] Catherine M. Wallace, "Consumerism and Christian Community," *Anglican Theological Review* 85, no. 3 (2003): 581–588. *ATLA Religion Database with ATLASerials*, EBSCOhost (accessed May 29, 2014), 582.

[22] Wendy Tremayne, "Making Vs. Consuming: A Conversation with Wendy Tremayne" Swap-O-Rama-Rama, July 19, 2007, accessed March 8, 2012, http://www.youtube.com/watch?v=9t10W4FxRnI.

[23] Eric Liu and Scott Noppe-Brandon, *Imagination First: Unlocking the Power of Possibility* (San Francisco: Jossey-Bass Publishers, 2009), Kindle location 400.

[24] Mark Driscoll, "Seeker Vs. Missional—Part One," *Desiring God*, July 8, 2006, accessed April 5, 2012, http://www.youtube.com/watch?v=4Gi0jWNAe6M.

[25] Abraham, John Menuier blog.

who come to see what the church has to offer are looking to receive much in exchange for little commitment or accountability.

Mike Breen, author and creator of 3DM, a missional movement originating in the United Kingdom, states, "When there isn't challenge, it creates an easy culture where we service our clients. A gimmicks culture continues to want more gimmicks. What if we are low on invitation and high on challenge? It becomes all about the challenge and nothing about the invitation."[26] He concludes by saying there is normally a high turnover in the gimmicks culture because the invitation is hard to sustain. Clients will simply move on to another gimmicky church that offers what they want.

The consumeristic and attractional model is a departure from the gospel. If sources are right, then what emerge are shallow, attractional, gimmick-obsessed, and me-centered Christians whose primary concern is to fulfill their own privatized needs. This result is no fault of the culture but of the church for weakening its stance, watering down its gospel message, and scrapping its methodology.

Alan and Debra Hirsch, in their book *Untamed*, call the church to return to true discipleship. They write, "The fact that discipleship in the church is considered a somewhat lost art ought to disturb us profoundly."[27] They also define more clearly what discipleship is not. The enculturated, attractional, and seeker-sensitive church attempts its hand at discipleship. According to the Hirsches,

> On the odd occasions we have actually managed to engage in some form of discipleship, we have tended to limit it to issues of personal spirituality (prayer times, Bible study, God's leading, tithing, etc.) and not conceive of it as something that has direct ramifications beyond the individual's privatized sensibilities. But discipleship

---

[26] Mike Breen, "Practicals for Discipling People Like Jesus Did" (presentation at Verge 2012, Austin, TX, February 29, 2012).

[27] Alan Hirsch and Debra Hirsch, *Untamed: Reactivating a Missional Form of Discipleship* (Grand Rapids, MI: Baker Books, 2010), Kindle location 68.

in the way of Jesus is surely much more comprehensive than that.[28]

In light of current descriptions of a me-centered Christianity, their statement illuminates both cultural and modern church tendencies, one of which is to foster and support privatized notions of me Christianity. The Hirsches make their point even more clearly when they say,

> That we have cultivated an attenuated form of "designer" discipleship, a do-it-yourself spirituality that has little to say beyond the confines of the Christian community itself, only highlights the need to recover something a whole lot more vigorous than what we currently have.[29]

These authors reveal the tamed nature of the current church and call for a return to the untamed Jesus and gospel. Paul Santmire offers insight into the culture of consumerism,

> Arguably, consumerism is driving us to destruction. The BP drilling disaster in the Gulf of Mexico appears to be a dramatic case in point. This is the logic behind it: We must find the energy resources we think we need in order to sustain our consumer economy, and if that means undertaking increasingly dangerous interventions into the earth's ecosystems, so be it.[30]

When considering the influences that have contributed to not handing the Christian faith over, we must also examine some deep, internal theological shortcuts. In his short essay, "On the Transmission of Christianity," C. S. Lewis recognized the core issue before the church. He writes, "If the younger generation have never been told

---

[28] Ibid., Kindle location 69.

[29] Hirsch and Hirsch, *Untamed*.

[30] H. Paul Santmire, "From Consumerism to Stewardship: The Troublesome Ambiguities of an Attractive Option." *Dialog* 49, no. 4 (2010): 332–339. *ATLA Religion Database with ATLA Serials*, EBSCOhost (accessed May 29, 2014), 332.

what the Christians say and never heard any arguments in defense of it, then their agnosticism is fully explained."[31] Lewis asserted that the church's nonengagement with the next generation will ultimately create indifference to the Christian faith. An analysis by Whitney Bauman affirms what others have suggested. She writes, "We simply buy and consume our latest identity because the 'no-self' of postmodernity lacks integrity, essence, substance."[32]

Back to Honeybees

Consumerism has fractured the culture, created significant identity deficits, and affected the church's ability to disciple the culture. Consumerism divides strong community and has contributed to interrupting our ability to form and mature followers of Jesus. Discipleship takes work and enormous investment by the body of Christ. It's hard to engage in a meaningful way when other attractional forces at work distract us. We spend the bulk of our collective time and resources attempting to attract people to our worship, programs, and events. The means of the attraction takes center stage. As a result, the process of discipleship gets curbed for flashy numeric gains. The church's nursery has taken a hit.

If the brood nest of a hive is broken, the colony can't survive indefinitely unless there is intervention. In part, this book is an intervention. Hives and churches mostly collapse because there is a social collapse, which leads to missional and incarnational failure and overall identity crises.

This is where we are as a church. Just under the lid is the smell we wish were different. It would be easy just to close the lid and move on to the next hive. Most beekeepers are keenly aware of the smell of rotting larvae in the nursery. Most of the time it is due to disease that disrupts

---

[31] C. S. Lewis, "On the Transmission of Christianity," in *God in the Dock: Essays on Theology and Ethics* (Grand Rapids, Mich.: William B. Eerdmans Publishing, 1970), Kindle location 1318.

[32] Whitney Bauman, "Consumerism and Capitalism: The True Costs of Integrity." *Dialog* 49, no. 4 (2010): 263–264, accessed May 29, 2014, doi.10.1111/j.1540-6385.2010.00546.x.

brood rearing. We open the lid and see the social structure collapsing, the nursery in shambles, and minimal foragers returning with food.

A beekeeper can determine if the colony is healthy or unhealthy and can be saved or not by simply observing the front of the colony and lifting the lid. Diligent beekeepers will check colony health frequently in order to catch problems early. If caught early, most of the colony issues can be remedied. The make-it-or-break-it variable is if there is a high population of bees in the box. The bees can recover most of the time if their population is high. If there is an issue and their population is low, it might just be better to merge them with another colony.

Perhaps I'm overly hopeful about the future of the church and at the same time naïve about its recoverability. However, I believe the population in the church hive is high enough to recover and turn the corner to fruitfulness. I also recognize that the majority of my readers don't know anything about honeybees, except they can sting, pollinate, and make honey. Before moving on, let me introduce you to honeybees. I know you want to pop the top on the hive and take a look inside.

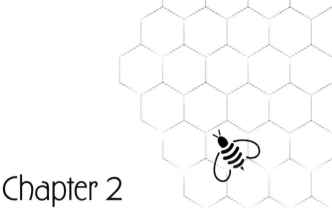

Chapter 2

Introduction to Honeybees (Apis Mellifera)

Author Margaret Feinberg, in *Scouting the Divine: My Search for God in Wine, Wool, and Wild Honey*, interviewed a commercial beekeeper. She "realized that bees and followers of God have something in common—each has specific role to play in order to effectively serve a greater purpose within the community (and it might change)."[33] In her pursuit of the divine, Margaret began to explore something she knew very little about: honeybees and their contribution to the human race. Using honeybees as the guiding metaphor, we will weave the metaphor with the practice of discipleship to give us an imaginative and authoritative approach to disciple making.

Honeybees (*Apis mellifera*) "have existed for at least 30 million years."[34] They live in a colonized order with thousands of bees. Scholar Thomas Seeley observes, "For a honeybee colony is an immense family consisting of the mother queen and her thousands of progeny. It is also true that the many thousands of attentive daughters (the workers) of the mother queen are, ultimately, all striving to promote her survival and reproduction."[35]

---

[33] Margaret Feinberg, *Scouting the Divine: my search for God in wine, wool, and wild honey* (Zondervan, 2009), Kindle location 1658.

[34] Thomas D. Seeley, *The Five Habits of Highly Effective Honeybees: And What We Can Learn From Them* (Princeton, NJ: Princeton University Press, 2010), Kindle location 35.

[35] Thomas D. Seeley, *Honeybee Democracy* (Princeton, NJ: Princeton University Press, 2010), Kindle location 87.

The queen is the center of a colony's life and "is longer than either the drones or workers, but her size, in other respects, is a medium between the two."[36] The large social group is comprised of drones (male bees from unfertilized eggs), female workers (infertile egg layers), and a single queen. The worker bees comprise the vast majority of the colony and do all the work in and out of the hive, with the exception of breeding and laying eggs. The drone bee's sole purpose is to mate with a queen.

The hatching queen will leave the colony for her nuptial flight. She will mate with numerous neighboring drones, eight to ten or more. The queen will store the sperm in her abdomen for her life and fertilize every worker egg she lays. Once mated, the queen will furiously begin to lay her eggs. "Each summer day, she monotonously lays 1,500 or so eggs needed to maintain her colony's workforce."[37]

Twenty-one days later, her first offspring begin to emerge from their cells. Every day after the twenty-first day, fifteen hundred eggs hatch so the colony population proliferates in a short period of time. The new queen that hatches and mates is the daughter of the queen she replaced. Prior to her birth, the mother queen swarmed with the young bees. The young queen is now left with the remainder of the colony of older bees and hatching infants. The younger bees that swarmed with the already fertile queen will live longer and be able to build a nest with the honey they took from the parent colony.

Swarming is a natural process to perpetuate and multiply the species. Honey is needed to produce the wax for the nest and storage. It is worthy to note that only young bees produce the wax that is needed to build hexagon cells. Older bees have lost the ability to make wax. You can see the importance of having young bees hanging around the nest.

A colony of bees carries out numerous responsibilities. One job is scouting. The scouts are female worker bees whose role is searching for a new home site. In a hive, many scouts are simultaneously searching for a new site in which to take up residence. Once the decision of a new home is made, a large portion of the colony will leave the parent colony for their

---

[36] Moses Quinby, *Mysteries of Bee-Keeping Explained* (New York: C. M. Saxton, Agriculture Book Publisher, 1853), Kindle location 543.

[37] Seeley, *Honeybee Democracy*, Kindle location 96.

new home. Swarming is an instinctive process designed to keep the colonies multiplying and perpetuating their kind. Beekeeper and author Brett Jones identifies some reasons honeybees swarm: "1. Overpopulation or congestion in the hive. 2. An imbalance between old and young worker bees. 3. The hive is often overheated and the bees are unable to adequately ventilate."[38]

However, instead of letting the bees swarm, beekeepers will sometimes intervene and stimulate the colony's growth and then split the hives to make more colonies. Late beekeeper Cliff Thomas called this "making set-outs."[39] Beekeepers will also replace the parent hive and new colony with new queens. Younger queens lay more eggs, which helps the population increase.

One of the honeybee's roles in creation is to pollinate commercial crops and flowers. Studies show "honey bees are the most economically valuable pollinators of agricultural crops worldwide."[40] Other researchers affirm the "insect pollination is an important ecosystem service to agriculture, improving production in 75% of global crops [1], including many important sources of nutrients in the human diet [2], and contributing an estimated 153bn to global agricultural crop value."[41]

However, they are not just to serve humanity through pollination and honey production. They are also an illustration of divine purposes, plans, and systems. Honeybees speak to the interconnection of every living thing and to the praise of their Creator. Michael O'Malley writes, "The organizing theme of the hive is that everything is done for the good of the whole, and the community is central to the operation of the colony."[42]

---

[38] Brett Jones, *Apiculture and Beekeeping Simplified* (Salt Lake City: Alpha One Publishing, 2012), Kindle location 1425.

[39] Cliff Thomas (1923–2007) is my grandfather. I learned beekeeping from him. Cliff used the phrase "making set-outs" to indicate splitting hives.

[40] Deborah A. Delaney, "Genetic Characterization of U.S Honey Bee Populations," (PhD diss., Washington State University, 2008), 1–99, August 5, 2014, Open access.

[41] Tom D. Breeze et al., "Agricultural Policies Exacerbate Honeybee Pollination Service Supply-Demand Mismatches Across Europe," *PLoS ONE* 9(1)(2014): 1–8, September 8, 2014, http://www.plosone.org/article/info%3Adoi%2F10.1371%2Fjournal.pone.0082996.

[42] Michael O'Malley, *The Wisdom of Bees: What The Hive Can Teach Business About Leadership, Efficiency, and Growth* (New York: Penguin Group, 2010), Kindle location 30.

The honeybee exists for the betterment of the colony and gives its life for the community. As a "true social system, every bee works and sacrifices to produce an organization that is greater than the sum of the parts."[43] Teresa Morgan in *Literate Education in the Hellenistic and Roman Worlds* writes, "Bees were widely used as an image of a model society. They are described as perfectly social creatures who subordinate their individuality to the harmonious whole."[44]

All three Synoptic Gospels include the lessons of self-denial, suffering, and the following of Jesus. Jesus told his listeners, "Whoever wants to be my disciple must deny themselves and take up their cross daily and follow me. For whoever wants to save their life will lose it, but whoever loses their life for me will save it" (Lk 9:23–24 NIV).

Such lessons are a part of community life. In the introduction to *The Disciple Making Church*, writer Bill Hull observed, "The church systems we have set up protect those who profess from the intrusion of discipleship. We say it is okay to be a part of our churches without a requirement to follow Jesus, again because our gospel requires nothing of its recipients."[45]

Hull is spot-on with his remarks. The Christianity we have been proclaiming is a crossless faith. That is, we have removed the difficult portions that have to do with commitment, accountability, and sacrifice. Without them, what sort of Christianity are we left with? The answer is what we are currently living with.

In a bee colony, every act is done for the benefit of the whole, and every honeybee is willing to make a sacrifice and deny self for the sake of the mission. The internalized values of the church should be no different. These are the values Jesus taught and practiced, even to death. "Jesus makes no apologies for his strong words. He wants people to be clear about what they are signing on for."[46]

---

[43] Ibid.

[44] Teresa Morgan, *Literate Education in the Hellenistic and Roman Worlds* (Cambridge: Cambridge University Press, 1998), 263.

[45] Bill Hull, *The Disciple-Making Church: Leading a Body of Believers on the Journey of Faith* (Grand Rapids, MI: Baker Books, 2010), 14.

[46] Kyle Idleman, *Not a Fan: Becoming a Completely Committed Follower of Jesus* (Grand Rapids, MI: Zondervan, 2011), 65.

Beekeeping is more than a descriptive metaphor for the church and the process of discipleship. Beekeeping is a revelation of the nature and systems of God that inform our understanding of God and practice of discipleship. Presented here is a discipleship story right out of God's creation. The aim of a theology of beekeeping is to help the church return to incarnational and relational discipleship. Can we recover something sweet from the collapsing lion of the church? There is something pure and sweet in the midst of the dying and decaying lion of Sampson's riddle. The same can be said for the modern day church. Just below the surface of a seemingly troubled church is a process which can resurrect the body of Christ.

The reality of where the church is reminds me of a family story relayed to me. Perhaps this story will help us understand something about where we are as a church and how we recover. In 1911, a wild man was found in a cattle barn in Oroville, California, attempting to eat a calf. As you can imagine, this grabbed the attention of residents and local law enforcement. The wild man was starving to death and had made his way to the livestock barn. It didn't take long to discover this wild man was a Native American.

As it turned out, people who stumbled across this Native American's camp had ransacked it. They took his bows and arrows, his means of hunting. He was literally starving to death in the mountains, and he was in search of food. The Native American's name was Ishi, and he had lived alone for many years when he was discovered. When they discovered him in 1911, they discovered the last "wild" Native American.

Many from the University of California studied Ishi's ways, culture, methods, and life. After spending most of his life in seclusion, his immunity was ill-prepared to deal with the onslaught of viruses and infections. He was sick a lot. Ishi finally died in 1916 from tuberculosis. The final five years of his life were spent telling the story of his ways and people. Researchers learned a lot from Ishi about the culture of his people.

Like Ishi, the modern church is starving to death. Our tools and means for hunting have been removed from our camps and lost to us. We are desperate for some kind of food that will nourish our faith. So much so, we have wandered around the countryside, trying to find the next gimmick to ease our hunger pains. Like Ishi, there is a real treasure in our sacred past. There is a culture lost to us that, once recovered, will help nourish the future church. The practice and culture of discipleship can offer a hopeless people resurrection.

Ishi taught researchers a lot about his people. He passed on his sacred legacy in just a few short years. Likewise, discipleship is a sacred culture that needs to be passed on to the next generation. Beekeeping also needs to be passed down to future generations.

I originally learned beekeeping from my grandfather. However, my father has taught me more than he knows about how to keep these tiny, little insects. He learned how to keep bees from his father (my grandfather), who learned to keep bees from his father (my great-grandfather), Arthur Banta. Arthur became interested in beekeeping while attending the University of California at Davis.

Interestingly, my great-grandfather, Arthur Banta, our patron beekeeper, knew Ishi, no doubt meeting him through the University of California. A priceless treasure was discovered in the foothills of Northern California when Ishi was discovered. Will the church as we know it, like Ishi, be able to survive the infections and viruses the culture passes on to us, or will this very lost and collapsing church rediscover the story of discipleship?

As it turns out, something strong and sweet is emerging from the dying lion of the church. That something lost to us is just beneath the hide of the lion. There is sacredness there, if we are willing to step a little closer and take a look.

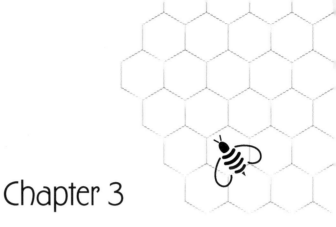

Chapter 3

The Sacredness of Bees and Theology of Beekeeping

Honeybees have been worshiped by ancient cultures and used symbolically throughout history. Many cultures, including Christianity, have deemed honeybees sacred and used them as powerful examples of organization and productivity. One such example is "the Papal Tiara that has been used since the thirteenth century is made to resemble a beehive."[47] Austin Fife points out,

> In the Middle Ages beekeeping became a near monopoly of the monastic orders and canonical fiefs, despite the efforts of the peasantry to protect their only source of sweets—their bees—by rites, beliefs, and practices which wedded them to the family more closely than any of the other domestic animals.[48]

These insects have intrigued many and frightened many more. Modern-day researchers explore the wonder of honeybees and attempt to grasp their overall significance. Lisa Jean Moore and Mary Kosut observe, "We continuously grapple with the human practice of seeing bees as signifying something else, through metaphor, and approach an

---

[47] Bodog Felix Beck, *Honey and Health: A Nutrimental, Medicinal and Historical Commentary* (New York: R. M. McBride and Co., 1958), 714–715.

[48] Austin Fife, "Christian Swarm Charms from the Ninth to the Nineteenth Centuries Author(s)," *The Journal of American Folklore* 7, no. 304 (1964): 154–159, accessed August 20, 2014 http://www.jstor.org/stable/537564.

ontological reckoning with the insect."[49] This research is a reckoning and reconciliation with the honeybee insect.

One of the earliest sources for understanding the nature of honeybees is found in a poem by Publius Vergilius Maro (Vergil). R. M. Millington translated the poem into English in 1870. Vergil was born in October 70 B.C.

The Fourth Georgic of Vergil

But when the golden sun has put to flight
And driven winter down, when summer light
Has once again unloos'd the frost bound sky,
At once through grove and woodland glade
They fly;
The sweets from all the gay-hued flowers cull,-
A tiny draught sip from the streams; or, full
Of some deep joy, keep all their nestlings warm
And give them food; then skilfully they form
New cells, and frame the clinging honey-store.
When from the hive thou see'st the Swarm forth
Pour,-
When like dim clouds that float through summer air,
Amaz'd, thou gazest at their flight, take care
To watch them closely; they will ever fly
To some sweet stream, some leafy canopy,
And there upon the branches of some tree
Rub thou the scent of plants now told by me:
Bruis'd balm and common honey-wort:-the sound
Of bells or clashing steel stir up:-around
Beat loud the cymbals of great Cybele.
Then gladly will they settle of the tree

---

[49] Lisa Jean Moore and Mary Kosut, *Buzz: Urban Beekeeping and the Power of the Bee* (New York: New York University Press, 2013), 18.

Thus rubb'd, and gladly in the bee's own way
Hide in the hive's recess."[50]

The poem is about the nature and seasons of beekeeping. The section of the poem above indicates the spring swarming season of honeybees. In poetry form, Vergil supplies one of the earliest manuals for beekeeping. "When Vergil wrote about the bees in the Georgics, he enters into their life so heartily that we feel he must have been brought up among them."[51] Hilda Ransome also observes,

> What veneration and yet what fear these tiny creatures excited in man! They exercise a fascination even on those who fear their sting, and all who tend them have quite a peculiar love and regard for them which they do not feel for other animals and which is a bond of union between all beekeepers; they feel that they belong to a fraternity which reckons Vergil among their number.[52]

Vernon Kellogg wrote a children's novel about the new life that one can have through the story of a honeybee. The life stages of a honeybee are accurately captured through the experiences of "Nuova"[53] (new bee).

William Shakespeare also understood the intrinsic value of honeybees. He writes,

So work the honey bees,
Creatures that by a rule in nature teach

---

[50] Vergil, *The Fourth Georgic of Vergil, Containing An Account of the Treatment of Bees, The Story of Aristaeus and His Bees, The Episode of Orpheus and Eurydice; and An Article on The Gladiators*, trans. R. M. Millington (London: Printed By W. H. and L. Collingridge, 1870), lines 77–99.

[51] Hilda M. Ransome, *The Sacred Bee in Ancient Times and Folklore* (Boston and New York: Houghton Mifflin Company, 1937) 84.

[52] Ibid., 19.

[53] Vernon Kellogg, *Nuova or The New Bee: A Story of Children of Five to Fifty* (Boston and New York: Houghton Mifflin Company, 1920), 1.

The art of order to a peopled kingdom;
They have a king and officer of sorts;
Where some like magistrates, remain at home,
Others like merchants venture trade abroad;
Others like soldiers armed in their stings,
Make boot upon the summer's velvet buds;
Which pillage they with merry march bring home
To the royal tent of their emperor:
Who, busied in his majesty, surveys
The singing masons building roofs of gold,
The civil citizens kneading up the honey,
The poor mechanic porters crowding in
Their heavy burdens at this narrow gate,
The sad-eyed justice, with his surly hum,
Delivering o'er to executor pale
The lazy yawning drones. [54]

Children's stories, poems, histories, and even hymns have been written to express the importance of honeybees. A hymn by Isaac Watts is a good example of a more modern praise of the honeybee. He wrote,

How Doth the Little Busy Bee

How doth the little busy bee
Improve each shining hour,
And gather honey all the day
From every opening flower!
How skilfully she builds her cell!
How neat she spreads the wax!
And labors hard to store it well
With the sweet food she makes.
In works of labor or of skill,
I would be busy too;
For Satan finds some mischief still

---

[54] Shakespeare, *Henry V*, I, ii, lines 187–204.

For idle hands to do,
In books, or work, or healthful play,
Let my first years be passed,
That I may give for every day
Some good account at last.[55]

Saint Ambrose is one of the recognized saints of the Catholic Church. The biography and legends surrounding Ambrose are worthy of inclusion here.

The title *Honey Tongued Doctor* was initially bestowed on Ambrose because of his speaking and preaching ability; this led to the use of a beehive and bees in his iconography, symbols which also indicate wisdom. This led to his association with bees, beekeepers, chandlers, wax refiners, etc.[56]

The folklore and legend surrounding Saint Ambrose maintain that, when he was an infant, a swarm of honeybees landed on his face and emitted a drop of honey on his tongue. As a result, he was dubbed the patron saint of beekeeping.

Ambrose was prepared for a public career in the Roman Empire by the best training available, which included legal studies, and that he carried on administrative work for some time in which he became familiar with legal usage, so that even after his change of profession it was but natural that the legal influence should be apparent.[57]

---

[55] Isaac Watts, "How Doth the Little Busy Bee," *poets.org*, accessed November 20, 2014, http://www.poets.org/poetsorg/poem/how-doth-little-busy-bee.

[56] Patrons of the Faith, "Patrons of Bees," accessed September 2014, http://saints.sqpn.com/patrons-of-bees.

[57] Lois Miles Zucker and S. Ambrosii De Tobia, "A Commentary, with an Introduction and Translation," (PhD diss., Catholic University of America, Washington, D.C., 1933), 19.

As it turns out, God had different plans for Ambrose.

Honeybees have also been a great example of virtue and productivity. Sister M. Theressa of the Cross Springer indicates, "Virginity is an enclosed garden and a heap of wheat, and virgins are exhorted to be like bees in continence and in industry."[58] The continence of bees to virgins originates with Vergil.[59]

One of the best sources for the sacredness of honeybees in pre-Christian and Christian culture is a dissertation by Austin Fife. Fife writes about the sacredness and unifying theme found throughout history. He writes,

> While there is a certain variety in the earliest existing forms of bee, honey, and wax lore, there is a single unifying concept that has dominated the greater part of the world's folklore and mythology concerning them. That unifying concept is that the bee and the two extremely useful products which it furnishes for mankind—honey and beeswax—are sacred objects. This universal concept of the sacredness of bees, honey, and wax seems to result essentially from the utility of honey as a food for man.[60]

Beekeeping has been in existence for centuries.

> The earliest absolute proof of domestic bee culture is not to be found, however, until 2600 B.C. On a wall of the Temple of the Sun built by Ne-User-Re (fifth dynasty) at Abusir, Egypt, there is a relief which illustrates an advanced type of bee culture that could have existed only after several centuries of earlier and more primitive culture.[61]

---

[58] Sister M. Theressa of the Cross Springer, "Nature-Imagery in the Works of Saint Ambrose," (PhD diss., Catholic University of America, Washington, D.C., 1931), 137.

[59] Ibid., 75.

[60] Fife, 485.

[61] Austin Fife, "The Concept of the Sacredness of Bees, Honey and Wax in Christian Popular Tradition," (PhD diss., Stanford University, June, 1939), 169.

Fife also observes,

> Let us remember, also, that the use of the bee as a symbol
> of kingly power, which dates from the first Egyptian
> dynasty, implies a knowledge of the natural history of
> bees which could scarcely be obtained except from a
> close observation of the social life of bees, and hence in
> artificially prepared hives.[62]

Honeybees have inspired, been symbolically used, and labeled
sacred. Fife observes,

> The cult of the sacred honey was expressed in the concept
> of its heavenly origin, in its prestige as the food and drink
> of gods, in its use as an article of sacrifice to gods and to
> the dead, in its use, frequently with milk or butter, in birth,
> circumcision, marriage, purification and death rites, in its
> medical uses, in embalming and as a bringer of the gifts of
> wisdom, eloquence, prophecy, and the poetic arts.[63]

In early Christian rites of passage, honey was a powerful symbol of
hope. "One of the oldest and at the same time one of the most intimate
incursions of honey into the Christian cult is its use, mixed with milk,
in the first communion of the neophyte performed immediately after
his entrance into the Church through baptism."[64] Fife also notes, "The
mixture of milk and honey symbolizes the land of promise."[65]

Austin Fife, Hilda Ransome, and few other minor contributors
are on a short list of persons who have researched and written about
the history, symbolism, and sacredness of bees in numerous cultures.
Among the sources, Austin Fife produced one of the best. His and
others' contributions have aided in developing a theology of beekeeping
that informs the practice of discipleship.

---

[62] Ibid., 22.

[63] Ibid., 485–486.

[64] Fife, *Sacredness of Bees*, 169.

[65] Ibid., 170.

Theology of Beekeeping

To help us transition to a theology of beekeeping, a passage from Austin Fife's dissertation will be included. The passage highlights the connection of the Hebrew people with the sacredness of bees. Like the sweet symbolism found in the biblical story of Samson and his lion, we find a similarity in the two Deborahs in the Old Testament. Fife writes,

> The most interesting Old Testament tradition about the bee is contained in the legend of Deborah, the prophetess and judge of the Jewish people. Her story presents the clearest example of the metaphorical nature of the Hebrew tradition, and most surprising parallels with the Greek bee-nymph and bee priestess lore. Now first of all we must remember that the name Deborah is the Hebrew word for bee, and that is derivative of the word debash, "honey".
>
> In the first place, there are two Deborah's in the old testament: Deborah who was the nurse for Rebekah, and she who was a prophetess and judge." Genesis 24:59. A woman whose name is "bee" is the nurse of the lovely Rebekah and accompanied her when she went away to become the bride of Isaac. This nurse is an important enough personage to have her name mentioned, her death and burial recorded, and to have a river and the oak tree beneath which she was buried named after her. Moreover, it is significant that this bee-nurse (i.e., nymph) is buried under an oak tree.[66]

The two Deborahs are significant personalities in the Old Testament, as Fife suggests. Fife also gives us additional commentary on the Deborahs and unlocks the embedded symbolism and sacredness of honeybees. He writes,

---

[66] Fife, 156–157.

But let us now examine the story of the other Deborah, for it will furnish us with equally significant facts. Here we have a "bee" who is a prophetess and judge of the Hebrew people. She dwelt under a sacred tree, although in this case it is a palm not an oak. Like her predecessor the nurse of Rebekah, she is from Beth-el. And at this point it is interesting to note (Genesis 28:19) that Beth-el, which means "the house of God" was a city whose former name was Luz, "almond tree" and had been changed by Jacob. The Children of Israel come up to her for judgment; she is inspired by God to incite the children of Israel to war against the Canaanites, is successful in the campaign, and sings a song of triumph and praise of God when the battle is over. No legend I have found is more filled with bee mythology and bee symbolism than this, and few Biblical episodes have such a close parallels in Indo-European tradition. Here we have a bee that is an intermediary between God and his people, a bee that is a prophet and sage, and a bee that is endowed with a gift of poetry and eloquence.[67]

The two Deborahs are powerful stories that reconnect the sacredness of bees with human roles, namely nurse and prophet. The honeybee is born and assumes its first role as cell cleaner. Not long after that, the new bee takes on the role of a nurse. The first Deborah (bee) is a powerful and needed nurse and guide to Rebecca. Said another way, the first Deborah is a mentor, guide, and a maturing agent in the life of Rebecca. Drawing an inference, Deborah is a disciple maker. In short, the bee is a symbolic guide.

The second Deborah is a mouthpiece for God. As Fife suggests, the prophet Deborah (bee) is an "intermediary between God and his people." It is suggestive that honeybees are intermediaries between God and us. Through honeybees (God's creation and revelation), we can know God and his will. Said another way, God speaks to us through honeybees!

---

[67] Fife, *Sacredness of Bees,* 158–159.

While the two Deborahs are powerful symbols, where they were from is even more symbolic. Both hailed from Bethel, which, as noted above, means "house of God." However, also noted above, the former name of Bethel was Luz (almond tree). The house of God is the almond tree. The Deborahs (honeybees) are from the house of God or almond tree. Even more revealing is almond trees have to be pollinated by honeybees in order for them to produce. Most migratory beekeepers move their bees all across the United States to California to pollinate the vast almond orchards. The house of God or almond tree (church) is pollinated with the word of God by the Deborahs (honey bees). The Bible is an endless metaphorical amusement park for our enjoyment.

The sacredness of honeybees is found across the breath of scripture. What we find is honeybees take a revelatory role in scripture. God has shared something of his nature, purposes, and procedures through this amazing little insect. The scriptures uncover just how deep and broad the connection really is. You have sampled a small portion of this connection.

Just beneath the hide and attached to the ribs of the dead lion is the buzz of our Creator. Bees are sacred and point to the remarkable mind and hands of our Lord. There are indeed some sweet drippings from the comb. There is hope for our ministries, church, and life with God. There is also a death we have to reckon with.

Under every rock and tucked away in the most unusual places, we discover God's secrets and divine connection. Honeybees, as it turns out, are not a trifling insect. They are divinely made and purposed. They are powerful symbols and a revealing source of the power and nature of God.

A theology of beekeeping has its origin in a Trinitarian understanding of God. God is one in three persons. God the Creator showed up through his creation in the person of Jesus to save his creation. In ancient literature, Jesus Christ has been referred to as "the bee" and his mother "the paradise of delight on which the bee feeds."[68] Jesus Christ (the bee) is the "intermediary between God and the people."[69]

God the Creator showed up in God the Son to reconcile his lost

---

[68] James George Roche Forlong, *Faith of Men: A Cyclopedia of Religions* (London, 1906), 271.

[69] Fife, *Sacredness of Bees*, 159.

creation. Jesus was the new Deborah of his age and for all time. God the Spirit sustains and empowers creation's renewal. Jesus Christ then is the Sacred Bee, which gives life to his colony. Like Deborah, Jesus is the master disciple maker and intermediary between God and his people.

The theological hinge is the unchanging nature of God's essence. The very system God created and used to mature life that he had made, he also used to mature the followers he had chosen in the gospels. God's process for maturing life is revealed in creation generally and honeybee colonies specifically. The claim is Jesus's process for maturing followers is a mirrored image of creation, both past and present.

Those desiring to follow Jesus Christ can learn how to do that, partially through observation of honeybees. Equally, those wanting to learn about the environment, love, connection, sacrifice, commitment, and so on can do so by observing honeybees. A theology of beekeeping isn't adequate, in and of itself, to save humankind apart from the special revelation that is Jesus Christ. However, the study of honeybees is revelatory and gives us a window to view the Creator and his system for maturing life. A theology of beekeeping leads us to see the source of love and connectivity of God and his people.

According to Genesis 1, God commanded his creation "to be fruitful, multiply and fill the earth" and gave them a system that perpetuates life. Genesis 1 also records God spoke the world into existence. Creation then is the spoken word of God. Honeybees, by extension, are God's living word and sustained by the power of God the Spirit.

Honeybees were created to pollinate and feed the planet, provide honey for consumption, and provide a window to view the nature, wonder, and systems of God. The honeybees and disciples of Jesus will undergo the same process to become fruitful and mature foragers for God. Disciples of Jesus, like honeybees, will mature by means of accountable and highly relational community and their incarnational presence in the world. This maturity leads to multiplication.

The story of Samson in the Bible ranks right up there in prized literature. It is a tale of a very strong guy who is mighty. The secret to his strength is his long hair. Cut the hair; lose the strength. Samson is representative of what Israel could be if they had long hair or if they trusted in God. The lesson that emerges from the narrative is "God is our hope and strength."

The lion is also representative of the Hebrew people. Like Samson, the lion is long-haired and strong. However, the lion Samson bested is weak. The nation of Israel was defeated and laid to waste. God had other plans for them though. The riddle is about the hope that is nestled within the lion. There is hope for a very defeated and broken nation.

Could the lion be symbolic of the modern-day church? Is it possible that, out of the dead or dying lion, something strong and sweet may emerge that will give life to the body of Christ and his world? Is it possible that, out of our failure, Jesus, the Great Bee, could resurrect his creation to new and abundant life? Out of the belly of the lion, the cradle of life emerges and provides us something strong and sweet. The modern church has to answer the Samson riddle.

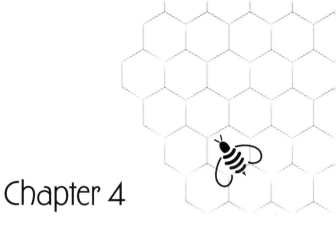

Chapter 4

The Cradle of Life/Hexagon of Discipleship

For since the creation of the world God's invisible qualities, his eternal power and divine nature, have been clearly seen, being understood from what has been made, so men are without excuse.　　—Romans 1:20

The imaginative answer to the problem of Church Collapse Disorder that plagues the church can be found in the cradle of life. Oddly, the answer to Samson's riddle begins with the holy shape of a hexagon. Did you know that a hexagon is a holy shape, a life-giving form? It is the shape of the cells in a honeybee hive. Thousands upon thousands of small hexagon shapes line the inside of a colony. They are all perfectly symmetrical and made with wax secreted from the bees. Every ounce of pollen and honey is stored in these hexagon-shaped cells. In addition to food storage, the cells are also the cradle of life for the colony. Every egg the queen lays is deposited at the bottom of a hexagon. The nursery of a colony also contains multiple thousands of this hexagon-shaped cell.

Creation contains that seed of imagination that enlightens the practice of discipleship. Considering Christ as a dying seed that brings forth life when planted in the garden tomb is a metaphor for God's connections and systems in his created order. In *In Plain Sight: Seeing God's Signature throughout Creation*, Dr. Charles R. Gordon magnifies this connectivity and reveals the Creator's divine design in what he calls "the Lattice of Life." He writes,

My parents built a chicken coop out of traditional chicken wire lattice, which has a distinctive pattern of interconnected hexagons. I did not realize it then, but this pattern is the most fundamental building block of life. Carbon Molecules naturally form the same hexagonal shapes that can connect like that chicken wire lattice. Carbon, the same substance in humble pencil lead and the most beautiful diamond, is crucial to life. The reason why is because the bonds carbon molecules form are uniquely suited to form the basis of organic chemistry, and even DNA itself. And this pattern doesn't stop there. We see it repeated in honeycombs (how do bees know how to make those?) and in the covering of the eye in the cornea.[70]

Dr. Gordon creates awareness of the divine designer and the interconnectedness of all of life. Genesis tells us God created man from the dust of the earth "and that's what carbon powder is—dust!"[71] The dust of the earth is the cradle of life and is in the shape of a hexagon.

The Hebrew image of God in creation is the image of a potter sitting at a wheel. The Divine Potter reaches down to the ground and scoops up the earth. The dirt is placed on the spinning wheel. As the wheel begins to turn, the Divine Potter begins to form man into his image. No doubt, a sprinkle of water is added in order to work with the clay. The dirt the potter picks up is carbon powder. Man is created out of the holy shape of a hexagon.

The center of life and activity for a beehive is the place where life breaks through. Emerging from the hexagon-shaped, encased cells is the future of the colony. Baby bees have to chew their way to life. The struggle they go through and nutrients they eat on their way out strengthen them for the work of the colony.

God created life from a hexagon and remade it through one. The

---

[70] Charles R Gordon. *In Plain Sight: Seeing God's Signature throughout Creation* (Tyler, TX: 2009), 159.

[71] Ibid., 160.

same God who created the world out of a shape took the shape of humanity. God became a member of his creation. His creation had a hard time recognizing him though and ultimately killed him and laid him in the earth. Out of this hexagon tomb, life emerged like a tender shoot. What was denied our first parents in the garden of Eden was now available to all humanity: the Tree of Life. Jesus, like a seed, died and was planted in the hexagon, the earth. What emerged from this shape was life.

The modern church lost its hexagon, in that it lost the hexagonal nursery of life. It has failed to reproduce its kind. However, the dying or dead lion may offer some hope for the future. God created life and redeemed it, and he can resurrect it. The church isn't so far gone that God can't renew its life.

The divine shape of a hexagon represents birth and rebirth, life from death, and renewed hope. The hexagon tells of a divine process, where life emerges and breaks through painful barriers. The hexagon is a divine process or nursery to raise followers of Jesus. The problem is the modern church has lost the process and community necessary for maturing disciples.

The theme song to the 1980s sitcom, *Cheers*, as well as the show itself, speaks to our human need for community. We all long to be in a place where we are known and accepted, a location where everyone knows our name. One of the most famous theme songs in television history, the lyrics speak to our need to be known as human beings, a requisite we long for and find in any venue. The producers of *Cheers* created a show that struck the hearts of the listening audience, and the theme song brilliantly captured the theme of needing to be known in community. The song is so familiar and popular that I imagine you started humming the words.

The modern-day church has lost the vision of the ancient process of discipleship. As Dr. Gordon indicates, the covering of the cornea is the shape of a holy hexagon. Not only are we born through a hexagon and find life through this shape, we *see* through a hexagon. We are born and reborn spiritually through the lens of this holy shape. Our ability to see the world and the church with God's eyes will no doubt involve some corrective and hexagonal lenses.

To recognize the modern church lives in a bubble and has forgotten its holy mission to make followers of Jesus is a step in the right direction. Bursting the bubble and expanding our view is necessary to fulfill our mission. However, cataract surgery will be needed to recover the true nature of discipleship. Community, mission, incarnation, service, and sacrifice are the words and letters on an eye doctor's wall. Are they blurry to you? The hexagon of discipleship we are called to look through may have a cataract covering it.

If you recall, Jesus was always giving spiritual eye exams. The spiritual shape of many in Judaism was grim and in desperate need of a spiritual optometrist. On occasion, the Great Physician actually removed the impairments. Jesus once referred to Judaism's spiritual guides as blind guides. The modern-day church, like Judaism before it, needs corrective surgery to remove obstacles to our vision and repair our eyes. The hexagon of discipleship is available for us. It is just beneath the scales. Life is right behind those blurry lenses. Recovering the process to mature followers is found not only in the life of Jesus but also in his creation. Ultimately, the hexagon leads us to one of God's best metaphors: honeybees.

God created an insect that would be responsible for feeding the planet. Pretty amazing. Thankfully he didn't put us in charge of that task. We are only tasked with stewarding the hives. In truth, honeybees are the hinge of life. They are a metaphor that produces something life-sustaining and sweet, not only metaphorically but physically. Out of the bosom and blossoms of creation, God has supplied something sweet and nourishing for our spiritual lives.

Thousands of small hexagonal shapes line a beehive with thousands of workers emerging from these shapes each day. The queen of a colony will produce upwards of fifteen hundred eggs a day. She will lay them at the bottom of each hexagon-shaped cell. While she is doing that, thousands of workers are being born, cleaning cells of the colony, receiving food, eating, feeding larva, fanning to keep hive temperature regulated for brood rearing, foraging, scouting, and guarding the colony.

Once the queen lays the egg, it takes twenty-one days for it to hatch out and join the colony. Every day after twenty-one, fifteen hundred bees hatch out. The population proliferates rapidly in the spring as the hive prepares for the nectar flow. It takes six pounds of honey to make one pound of wax. The honey the bees collected previously is used to build a nursery of wax. The cost of honey is significant but necessary if the colony is to reproduce its kind.

Discipleship is a costly investment of a church's resources and time but a necessary one if the church plans on reproducing. In a hive, you must have the right temperature to raise bees. Equally, the church needs the right temperature of community and mission to raise and multiply its offspring. Perpetuation of the species is built within the DNA of every living thing. Disciples are no exception. We were called to make more, so Jesus said at the conclusion of the gospel of Matthew. We were meant to multiply life.

Who would have ever considered the creation and importance of the shape of a hexagon? God did. Adam took shape through the form of a hexagon. It is the shape God uses to bring life. Reimagined, this figure can be used to help renew life for the church. From the creation of man to the birth of baby bees, God's will to create life is accomplished and sustained through a hexagon. This holy shape is the lens that will help us see the God who made it all, sustains it all, and has connected it all. Within this holy shape is a divine system that governs all of life and discipleship.

Push and Pull

As mentioned previously, there are numerous roles in a colony of honeybees. The first job a bee has when it is born is cell cleaner. It cleans and prepares the hexagons for more life or food. But it doesn't keep this job for long before it graduates to the new assignment of nursery worker. This is where the push and pull comes into play. Every day, bees are being born and dying. For every crop of bees born, this pushes the ones born before to the outer fringes of a colony. The need of a colony to care for its young and forage for food are the two most important tasks a colony has. While ones being born behind them push newborn bees, the newborns are equally being pulled to the mission of the colony, that is, foraging for food, water, and propolis. Bees are not born in the nest and confined to a nursery all their lives. They are actually pushed and pulled to many different jobs. If newborns stayed in the nursery all their lives, they would never make foragers and would ultimately starve to death. Making mature foragers is the goal of a colony.

Brian Johnson wrote an informative essay on the different castes within a colony during the nectar and pollen-rich season. He identifies four castes within a colony: "cell cleaners, nurses, middle aged bees, and foragers."[72] Cell cleaners are responsible for cleaning duties and typically stay a week in this caste. Nurse bees care for feeding larvae and the queen and spend a week in nursery duties. Middle-aged bees are in this caste for twelve to twenty-one days. Their tasks range "from nest building and maintenance, to nectar receiving and processing, to guarding the nest."[73]

The final caste in a honeybee colony is forager and ranges from twenty-one days until death. Within this highly social and accountable caste system, bees are pushed and pulled. In so doing, they are transitioned from one caste to the other, mainly through the needs of a colony. Johnson observes, "Bees living in healthy colonies in the spring and summer undergo three caste transitions: cell cleaner to nurse, nurse to MAB, and MAB to forager."[74] The key word in Johnson's observation is "healthy." Unhealthy colonies with collapsing social structures confuse these castes. Unhealthy colonies lose the very system of push and pull, and unless they recover, they will eventually collapse.

The church colony is not all that dissimilar from a honeybee colony. The church was called to push and pull on the young in the nursery. However, we lost the art of pushing and pulling (discipleship). As a result, we never graduated disciples from the nursery because we lost the measure of accountability necessary to push and pull. The modern church is declining, by and large, because this holy process for maturing disciples is lost to us. Just under the lid of what we expect is a diminishing church lies the root of the problem and a revelation of what will help us recover. The problem and revelation from inspecting the hive is

---

[72] Brian Johnson, "Division of Labor in Honeybees: Form, Function and Proximate Mechanism," *Behav Ecol Sociobiol* 64(3)(2010): 308, accessed October 25, 2014, http://www.ncbi.nlm.nih.gov/pmc/articles/PMC2810364.

[73] Ibid., 308.

[74] Johnson, 310.

a deficiency in push and pull. We might feel the pull to be missional but aren't prepared for flight. We, like new emerging bees, are grossly underdeveloped and unprepared for the world God calls us to.

Growing churches are healthy. They are brooding and hatching out. Numerous programs, events, and electrifying worship experiences indicate health and fruitfulness. Just under the lid and upon close inspection, another symptom reveals itself. To check for brood health, beekeepers will pull out an inner frame from the middle of the hive at the bottom, the brood comb. It is basically the nest or nursery. It is the great revealer of the future.

Sometimes if disease is just beginning in a colony, a beekeeper may not detect it until there is already a decline in numbers. Through experience and to test the health of capped larvae, a beekeeper will grab a frame of brood and give it a close look from front to back. It may appear to be healthy but needs an even closer inspection. A wise beekeeper will test the capped brood by taking a piece of grass or a small stick and sticking it in the encased larvae. If you pull the stick or grass out and it looks dark brown instead of milky white, the colony has a disease called foulbrood.

Growing churches may look vital and healthy. Close inspection might reveal the process of discipleship (nursery) is really diseased or absent. Underdeveloped and immature followers of Jesus will fill the church colony. We can offer as many gimmicks, events, and programs we want to get people in the door, but if there is not accountable push and pull, we are not fulfilling the Lord's call to make disciples.

The hive might look numerically healthy, but just under the lid is a breakdown in the process of discipleship. The flash and growth will only be sustainable with more flash and gimmicks. If your church stops offering gimmicks, why would people come there? Most will leave there and shop for another tantalizing experience. The consumeristic world has brilliantly enculturated the citizenry to be shoppers, selectors, or consumers looking for the best deal, most serviceable church, and tantalizing experience. Several reasons the attractional church is declining is gimmicks are expensive, ultimately unsustainable, and don't produce deeply committed followers of Jesus.

Young bees need pollen to eat because it is rich in protein. Obviously they can't go get it themselves because baby bees' wings aren't fully developed yet. Foragers have to bring pollen to them. It is the forager's responsibility to collect nutrition from the field and bring it back to the colony so the nursery has food. It is the nursery's responsibility to prepare the bees to be foragers. It there is a social breakdown within the colony and the roles of bees are confused, the colony is heading toward collapse. A social breakdown may be the result of disease, pests, or loss of a queen.

The push and pull of a colony is needed within the context of the church as well. As a disciple of Jesus is being formed and grounded in a relationship with the Father through accountable measures, he or she is equally being pulled into the mission field, where he or she will learn to forage and sense God's activity in sight and smell. As new sources of God's activity are found, the disciple reports back to the church, and then the church joins the disciple in the field.

Jesus pushed his disciples into the mission field. Luke 9 and 10 record the push Jesus makes to mature his disciples. They are learning how to follow Jesus and make followers by actually being incarnational in God's mission field. This is Jesus's design to mature his disciples. Experiencing success and failure would be valuable in preparing his followers after his ascension to bear the good news of his life. Post-Pentecost, the power and working of the Holy Spirit would equally push and pull the disciples into the mission field. No doubt the need of the people would pull them to forage as the Spirit pushed them out of the upper room.

Honeybees are born in a push-and-pull environment, and this makes them producers. The system that governs their lives is the cradle of life for the world. Their unique system has six major components to it: incarnational nature, accountable community, clustering, education (breaching barriers), sacrifice, and mission.

A hexagon is a six-sided shape, and from this form, the cradle of life exists. Discipleship, as a process for maturing followers of Jesus, doesn't exist without these six sides. If any are missing from the dimension, the colony of the church will eventually collapse. If each of these is attended to in the life of a church, the maturity that leads to multiplication will happen. These sides will be the focus of the next several chapters.

It turns out that out of the very weak and dying lion—the cradle of life or the hexagon of discipleship—is emerging as something strong and sweet.

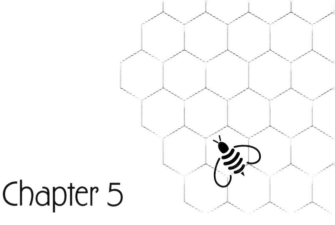

Chapter 5

The Dance of Discipleship

While discipleship takes the shape of a divine hexagon, it is equally a dance. It is an informative, transformative, and disciplined response to God's movement among us. Music ushers in our dancing and playing. In fact, all of creation dances and plays when the music of life starts. The image of two, young white-tailed deer playfully sparring comes to mind. Both are dancing around on their hind legs, leaning into one another. It is a beautiful sight to see. Two bear cubs rolling around and playing together is another example. A multitude of dancing, singing, and playing examples fills God's creation.

If discipleship is a dance, where does that leave the modern-day church? Most would answer that question with shuffling. We often shuffle around in a hurry, offering "dance" classes on how to be busy but unproductive. It's pretend dancing or playing. We offer numerous gimmicks and attractional programs and events in the modern-day church experience. Everything from bells-and-whistles programs to hip worship styles fill our buildings and worship spaces. We also offer many Bible studies without . Little by way of praxis accompanies our intense studies of the word. Very little is offered in the way of robust and accountable process for maturity. Brian Zahnd, in *Beauty Will Save the World*, makes an observation and offering when he suggests, "The Western church has had a four-century experiment with viewing salvation in a scientific and mechanistic manner, presenting it as a plan, system, or formula. It would be much better if we would return to viewing salvation as a song we sing."[75]

Our churches are not, for the most part, dancing to the music of discipleship. They're barely moving. God gave us one of the best metaphors in creation to help the church learn the importance of discipleship dancing. Make no mistake, disciple making is an eloquent dance, requiring form, play, discipline, and music. Learning how to dance to the music of discipleship is important if the church is interested in recovering and making deeply committed followers of Jesus. In this arrangement, Jesus is the lead singer, and we accompany his lead. In order to arrive at the music that will allow the church to dance and play again, we need to rehire our lead singer.

The mission of the church is to make disciples. Jesus was very clear about that mandate for his recently created church. He basically told his disciples to go make more (Mt 28:16–20). How did a young Jewish carpenter from Nazareth plan to keep his movement going? The answer is easy: make followers who could keep the news of Christ alive. The more challenging question is: what was his method? How did Jesus take the raw material he had handpicked and shape it into something that could accompany him in his music? The answer is as old as creation.

Let me suggest to you that creation, as the spoken word of God, offers numerous lessons and sessions on how to be a better dancer and person of play. The early chapters of Genesis share the story of God speaking the world *ex nihilo* (out of nothing). Obviously matter doesn't predate the Creator. God spoke words, matter came into existence, and life came to be. His creation is the spoken word and is living. The God who made the matter literally showed up through it and took on its nature. You know how the story goes. God was born among us to the process he had created. God experienced all we do (with the exception of sin), starting with womb life and coming through the birth canal. Mary pushed as a nurse bee pulled Jesus to the world he had made. If the incarnation doesn't astound you and reduce you and I to total awe and reverence, nothing will.

---

[75] Brian Zahnd, *Beauty Will Save the World: Rediscovering The Allure & Mystery of Christianity* (Lake Mary, FL: Charisma House Book Group, 2012), Kindle location 108.

Most rational people would agree there is a divine designer. And almost all Christians profess this God showed up through a virgin named Mary. The God of creation showed up for redemption in and through the fully human and divine Jesus. Let me offer a couple questions at this point. Would God use the same process to mature disciples that he uses to mature his creation? If so, what would that process be? The answer to that question is the focus of what remains.

When reading the story of Jesus, one finds the discipleship process alluded to in creation. Maturity, in any species, is forged through the experience of living, whether a fledgling chicken hatching from an egg or the same adult bird running for its life to survive a predator is necessary to mature the bird. Humans are no different. It explains why Jesus sent out the disciples two by two into the towns and villages Luke 9-10). Such an experience of success and failure would be a necessary prerequisite for future ministry. Experience is the great teacher. The process found in creation and Jesus's ministry to mature offspring is formative and can't be sidestepped. The process itself has a goal, maturity that leads to reproduction.

Author and preacher Barbara Brown Taylor, in *An Altar in the World*, identifies numerous practices, one of which is the practice of paying attention. She writes, "The practice of paying attention is as simple as looking twice at people and things you might just as easily ignore. To see takes time, like having a friend takes time. It is as simple as turning off the television to learn the song of a single bird."[76] To reimagine discipleship will require us to pay attention to not only our lead singer but also what he has made. What we will discover is an altar in the world. This altar, unlike any other, is living.

For the past several centuries, we have not been paying attention to one of the greatest metaphors or altars God has given. Tucked away in groves around the world and lining fields of flowering blossoms are one of the greatest gifts God ever gave his creation. What if I told you we could learn how to follow the Lord and subsequently deepen our faith by engaging God's living word of creation? What we will find is a wealth of

---

[76] Barbara Brown Taylor, *An Altar in the World: A Geography of Faith* (New York: HarperCollins, 2009), Kindle location 564.

knowledge and deeper connections than we could ever have discovered without creation's witness. Honeybees are an altar in God's creation.

Did you know there is dancing in the hive? Why did God make bees dance? Let me non-timidly suggest that God loves dancing and music! Foraging honeybees return from their nectar and pollen runs and drop off what they have collected to middle-aged bees. When a huge nectar flow starts, the foragers will return to let the rest of the foragers know its exact location.

This vital information is communicated through an intricate dance. The dancing bee makes numerous turns and up-and-down motions to freely communicate the exact location of food. Other foragers also communicate the information she shares. The information is freely provided for the advancement of the colony. The dance tells the directions.

Remember, the aim of a colony is survival and perpetuation of their species. All information is shared collectively for the advancement of the hive. A colony has a shared intelligence. They are a superorganism. There are no secrets or misappropriations of information. What the forager is sharing is good news.

This good news lies outside the bee box in the mission field. It is incarnational information. It is missional information. It is sweet music to the dancing forager. Other bees gather around the dancing bees to learn where the food is. The goal is to gather enough food to make it through winter. To fulfill their mission, this vital information is freely shared. Like an army, the foragers will head to the source by the thousands. Their need to survive mobilizes them. The pollen and nectar are stored and used to feed the colony when the time comes when sources are unavailable.

The shared information of the dancing forager is the key to life for the colony. So vital, if there is sudden loss of foragers communicating location of food, the colony will suffer. What would happen if the forager or scout didn't share vital information on their return to the colony? A more appropriate question for the church would be: what would happen in the church if no one paid attention to our dance of discipleship? Collapse?

The way many modern churches work is they are engaged in

meaningful information sessions (sermons, Bible studies, and so on). There is a lot of information given but little dancing. The institutional church largely ignores the foragers who do return and dance. I can't imagine that happening in a colony because they care too much about their future and mission to not respond. Transformation in a hive or a church happens when the information is shared through a dance. The dance is so impressive and charismatic that it pulls the observers out of the colony and into the mission field. The bees have one thought in mind, to fulfill the hive mission.

Unfortunately the modern church spends a lot of time comparing its ministry to other churches and competing for members. By offering stellar programming, amazing facilities, and exceptional and gifted staff, the church seeks to wow unsuspecting seekers with bigger and brighter. Do such means transform people into deeply committed, sacrificial, generous followers of Jesus Christ? I dare say they don't. Very little by way of discipleship is happening in these contexts. It can't because enormous time and resources are allocated to attractional endeavors. It is more about servicing our clients than making followers of Jesus.

Wrestling the Bears

Beekeepers in certain parts of the northern United States deal with the diseases, pests, and other issues facing beekeepers everywhere. However, northern beekeepers deal with one issue that beekeepers in the South don't have to contend with—bears. Bears can demolish a bee yard and make a mess of equipment. Typically after a bear comes through a bee yard and damages numerous colonies, a beekeeper has to put up an electric fence to attempt to keep the bear(s) from returning.

Most people think the bear is after the honey. I suspect *Winnie the Pooh* has ruined us, just like *The Bee Movie*. Bears are not after the honey. They are after the nutritiously rich calories at the center of the colony. You guessed it! They are after the brood chamber, or what we have been referring to as the nursery. The larvae are high in calories and will help the bears pack on pounds. A bee yard to a bear is a delicious, all-you-can-eat buffet.

Most of the time, an electric fence is not deterrent enough to keep the bear from coming in the yard. The beekeeper will have to find another way to deter the bear. Several years ago, a friend of mine named Joe Hagan used a phrase I will never forget. In reference to parents who have not prepared their children by sheltering them from the world, Joe remarked, "They have not taught them how to wrestle the bear."[77] The modern church has not wrestled the bear of consumerism. The modern-day bear has attacked our brood-rearing process.

Following a bear attack on a bee yard, numerous hives have been systematically dismantled and torn up. As you can imagine, a beekeeper walking into a bee yard following a bear attack might experience more than agitated bees. Bees are confused, and they are hanging on fence posts, the sides of other hives, and all around the bee yard and beyond. When I tell you it's a real mess, I mean it's chaotic. It's like the bees can smell the bear long after the animal is gone. When a beekeeper walks in, guess who gets confused for the bear? The beekeeper!

It takes several hours to fix a bee yard, salvage boxes and frames, collect the bees, and dump them back into boxes. The problems we face with the enculturation of Christianity, gimmicky programs and events, and an overall amnesia of the process of disciple making are the bears we will have to wrestle with. It will take time to put our bee houses back in order.

Like a colony of bees, the church is called to forage. To make disciples like Jesus did, the church needs to forage. We communicate that life-giving mission with the dance of discipleship. In fact, we learn how to follow and obey. It's hard for bees to dance when bears are knocking over their hives and destroying their future nursery potential. If the bear eats up the nursery of a hive, the mission is lost.

After a bear attack, bees are agitated and flying around confused. Our current church resembles the overly agitated and aimless colony. Our bees aren't dancing to discipleship; they are trying to survive the bears. It's hard to be proactive with our mission when we are reacting to cultural bears. It's a defensive or heel posture. When the colony of the church spends a bulk of its time, resources, talents, and energy dug in deep to defend its turf from the influence of the attacking culture,

---

[77] Joe Hagan, conversation with author, Whitehouse, TX, September 22, 2010.

something gets lost. Namely, that loss is our mission, our process of discipleship, and our future. The beehive becomes overly guarded to the point of unfruitfulness.

The colony of the church can't survive without being engaged in our mission to make disciples. The mission takes us incarnationally into the world to pollinate persons' hearts with the love of Jesus Christ. The posture of living life is advancement. The dance of discipleship is incarnational ministry. This movement takes us on the dance floor of life to join our lives with others. The problem is the church has forgotten how to disciple persons into mature followers of Jesus. It has forgotten how to be incarnational. The honeybee can reteach us how to forage again.

Honeybees were created for advancement and perpetuation of their species. It is hardwired within them. If the bees don't advance outside their colony, the hive will collapse on itself. If honeybees fail to collect protein-filled pollen, they can't raise young bees to maturity. Pollen is high in protein and needed. What deeply rich pollen are we offering to young followers of Jesus that will help them eventually mature into foragers? The mission of a beehive takes them into the field. It is vital they go in order to support the brood nest. The colony will not survive if it is not incarnational. Nor will it survive if it doesn't attend to the nursery.

Jesus's ministry was incarnational. God advanced into human history. The gospel of John records how God carried out his ministry, and burrowed into the human condition (Jn 1). Jesus spent his life not in an office in the temple or local synagogue. He spent his time and ministry out with the public and with unusual characters.

In training his disciples to maturity, Jesus sent them into the mission field to pollinate. Luke records Jesus's incarnational ministry approach in chapters nine and ten. How were the disciples going to learn how to make followers? By being out in the mission field, infusing their lives with others. Jesus intentionally sent them into the context of wolves with no provision other than trusting his word. They were to "carry no purse, no bag, no sandals" (Lk 10:4). He also told them to stay where they were welcomed and not to move from house to house. Jesus's methodology appears to be highly relational and concentrated on just a few.

No species can survive unless there is advancement and pollination. It is vital to the perpetuation of all living things. Any church wanting to take its people deeper won't do so without an incarnational presence in the world where their lives are melded with others in a highly relational way. The mission field desperately needs to be loved or, rather, pollinated. Theoretical pondering alone won't transform the society or church. Praxis is the great teacher. Jesus knew that in both creation and his public ministry.

In preparation for this book, I established a missional/incarnational ministry with my church's youth group. The goal was to start the process of making deeply committed followers of Jesus Christ by engaging the students in a vital mission to their community. A program was designed that focused on serving others rather than just showing up for food, fellowship, games, and a lesson. We constantly took them to serve their community. What we discovered is we were making maturing followers of Jesus. The end result was a stronger sense of community, deeper commitment to be incarnational, and a growing program. We were taking the youth and their families deeper, and the fruit was visible.

While discipleship is a lifelong endeavor to maturity, we were seeing evidence of maturity and fruit. The church was starting to dance to the music of discipleship, and it started with the youth department. Of course, there were challenges to changing the cultural story of the church. We often experienced pushback from persons and families when we asked for a deeper commitment.

The renewed emphasis on discipleship focused on a missional and incarnational posture started changing the church. Families in the church started seeing their children engaged in the community and dancing the dance of discipleship. We started seeing more bees foraging and pollinating the community.

When the music begins to play, dancing won't be far behind. Discipleship is both music and dancing. In the honeybee world, the music is the sights and smells when those first flowers begin emitting sweet smells and growing in the field. The good news is there are always flowers blooming in our mission field. We can see and smell the lives God is working on. The church is called to move beyond its walls of complacency to the flowering meadow of flowers that need to be pollinated. The interesting thing about flowers is they can't produce unless they are pollinated.

The maturity of the church is dependent upon its engagement with the community in mission. We call this pollination in the bee world. The flowers need pollinating, and the bees need the pollen. Neither can survive without the other. And that's the beauty of God's creation. All are dependent on the sacred other, including us. We pollinate the communities we live in with the love of God, but those communities are also the nourishing pollen we need to become faithful followers of Jesus Christ.

Pollinating Our Context

Historian and author Leonard Sweet once said that Christians were called to pollinate the world with the love of God. He didn't realize the impact of his statement and the connection he helped forge.

Honeybees are an invaluable asset to the cycle of life by their pollinating efforts. Not only do bees produce delicious honey and medicinal benefits to the human race, they also are responsible for our diet and the overall well-being of life on God's earth. I'm sure bees are not aware that their pollinating contribution is vital to life. I'm pretty sure they don't know they are pollinating when they leave their colony in pursuit of food for their hive. They have no inclination that, every time they land on a flower, collect its resources, and then subsequently land on another flower, they are pollinating. While we are aware of their unawareness, we become aware of God's meaningful ways. Just to think, God's ecology of the planet, a system of governance, hinges on an insect.

No doubt God created the seed, heat, light, moisture, and process of photosynthesis. He also created the insect that would be responsible to manage the process. Essentially what a honeybee does to a flower in pursuit of food is fertilize it. The numerous small hairs on the bee, in addition to pollen baskets on the bee's legs, pick up the protein-filled pollen. When a bee lands on a new flower, the pollen from another flower is brought to the new flower, and the female organ on the flower is pollinated or fertilized.

What bees have in mind when they leave the colony to become

foragers is collecting enough pollen and nectar to feed a growing brood nest and store enough food to make it through the winter. The colony can't be sustained without foragers. Baby bees grow up and become fully mature adults by eating the protein-rich pollen that foragers collect.

In the previous chapter, it was stated that the church has not attended the nursery of the church. The process of discipleship (nursery) matures young and growing bees. It does so with pollen collected from bees that were once in the nursery. If there is a breakdown in the nursery, it spells disaster and eventual collapse of the colony. Likewise, if there is a sudden loss of foragers, the colony will starve to death. A colony needs to attend to both nursery work and foraging in order to pollinate the world. Translated to the church, attending to the process of discipleship through a healthy nursery and mission orientation will make deeply committed followers of Jesus.

The influence of the church on the community of flowers will be minimized if the nursery is unattended, and this will affect our foraging efforts. We were meant to pollinate the world with the love of God, and this is the food our young and growing disciples need. If the church is not going to engage in some type of meaningful discipleship, then eventually church collapse disorder is forthcoming.

The church can return to the fields to which we are called. Great numbers of flowers in the world remain unpollinated without foragers. Remember, foragers are made through a nursery that pushes and pulls them to maturity. That's what a good and accountable community is supposed to do. In order to return to the fields God is calling us to and pollinate his world with the love of God, we need to reconsider how we organize and understand ministry. Where do we start to recover?

Alan Hirsch and Tim Catchim, in *The Permanent Revolution: Apostolic Imagination and Practice for the 21st Century Church*, recommend a new framework for ministry called APEST. Taken from Ephesians 4:1–16, APEST stands for Apostle, Prophet, Evangelist, Shepherd, and Teacher. While every piece of the APEST puzzle is necessary, the office of the evangelist is the catalyst. Gifted evangelists help recruit, network, and build community. Initially the church needs gifted evangelists to draw people into the community of faith. Hirsch and Catchim write, "From what we can gather from observation and Scripture, evangelists are always looking to create a positive encounter between people and the core message of the church, especially the gospel. Generally they spread the message and enlist others to the cause."[78]

The authors highlight the key role of the evangelist as "exceptional recruiters, social connectors and sharers of good news."[79] While the gifted evangelist is central in fostering recruitment, building community, and sharing the good news, he or she does not bear the burden of ministry alone. They are the front lines of transitioning a church. The AP and ST of APEST are also needed to help a church culture change to disciple making. While acknowledging the importance of each giftedness, the evangelist's gift is central to turning a church around.

Piggybacking on Hirsch and Catchim's work is Neil Cole. In *Primal Fire*, Cole writes, "Every now and then, a special surprise turns up in the lost and found box. In the church, that something special is the gifted evangelist."[80] Jesus was the great disciple maker and the most gifted evangelist who ever lived. Jesus was able to draw people in and help them make divine connections. He did so in community and context. Where do we start to recover in reclaiming our mission to make disciples? We solicit the help of the evangelists God has already provided and will offer. Most are not a part of the church, but they are living among us undiscovered.

Food for the church or a colony of honeybees is found in the field. Jesus modeled this in his constant movement from place to place. The gospels record Jesus's movement from village to village. Jesus lived quite literally in the context he was ministering. He taught his disciples, modeled kingdom truths to them, and kept them in the mission field. Jesus was on the go. He modeled how to pollinate the community and context to his followers. Jesus's young disciples grew to maturity through this high-protein diet.

The model of Jesus then is advancement. He demonstrated and lived incarnationally. This is the memory he left his disciples. They all

---

[78] Alan Hirsch and Tim Catchim, *The Permanent Revolution: Apostolic Imagination and Practice for the 21st Century Church* (San Francisco, CA: Jossey-Bass, 2012), 37.

[79] Ibid.

[80] Neil Cole, *Primal Fire: Reigniting the Church with The Five Gifts of Jesus* (Bonita Springs, FL: Tyndale House Publishers, 2014), 177.

record Jesus's movement and his incarnational tendency. Jesus is about advancement. He is deeply relational. He mentors and models honeybee behavior in that he advanced into his world. Why does the God-Man model honeybee behavior? It's simple. He made them, and every aspect of their lives is a reflection of his.

A type of ministry that seeks to only engage participants intellectually and not incarnationally or missionally is doomed. All theory and no praxis don't lead to transformation. No doubt Jesus challenged the disciples intellectually but did so in their context. Advancement into the foraging fields of life to pollinate the flowers is indicative of God's *modus operandi*, or MO. God's way is advancement, which provides nutritional food to mature young and old bees alike.

Many models of ministry are convoluted with endless cultural norms and practices. Those norms and practices didn't rise out of obscurity overnight. Generations of enculturation have had their impact on the pollinating or advancing nature of the church.

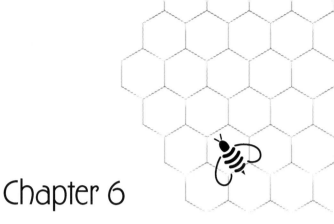

Chapter 6

Chew Your Way Through

Choosing to trust and follow Jesus Christ is at the heart of what it means to be a Christian. The decision to follow is one influenced by God's grace at work within each of us. It is grace that leads us to salvation and a life of pursuing relationship with the Lord. The decision to trust and obey will lead us to breaching a barrier. When one aligns himself or herself to Christ, there will no doubt be some adjustments. Numerous barriers like fear, loss, and education must be breached on the journey to maturity.

The nursery is the epicenter of every species God created. Life breaks through necessary and maturing boundaries, emerges from the hexagon, and blesses us. God created the nursery to mature the young. It is the place of struggle. As a child, I remember the first time I witnessed a chick being born in an incubator. It was amazing to see this little beak break the shell (boundary) of the egg. A big piece would break off, and there would be a momentary pause while the chick rested from the struggle to free itself from its enclosure. The process repeated until the newborn was finally free from its casing.

The chick sat for a while, got its bearings, and then huddled with the rest of the group. I remember reaching in to help the struggling chick and someone quickly told me not to. This person explained the chick needed to endure the exhaustion that comes from struggling. It would make the baby bird stronger to endure the process of being born.

Every creature needs to struggle and break through barriers if freedom and life are to be obtained. There are no exceptions, and the struggle continues throughout life. Humorously, humans attempt to secure a future without struggle, seeking with religious enthusiasm and justification more comfort, security, and shelter from struggles. Making life easier for our children does them a real disservice, but that's another book.

On the other side of the barriers is life. The original disciples had numerous barricades to go through in order to mature. They would not mature unless they chewed their way through the barrier, metaphorically speaking. Jesus constantly taught his disciples lessons he knew they needed. Such learning would push and pull them to real life.

One such example is Jesus's seminar out on the water. You recall the time Jesus came walking on the water and the disciples thought he was a ghost. When they realized it was Jesus, Peter wanted to come out to him. Jesus invited him to join him. Everything was going according to plan until a barrier fell in front of Peter. The wind and the waves distracted Peter, and he began to sink. Peter called on the Lord, and Jesus reached down to pick him up. They then climbed into the boat together. It was a teachable moment for the disciples and us.

Notice that Jesus didn't come walking on the land and wait for the ship to port. He purposely sent the disciples ahead of him. Neither did Jesus offer a seminar on the boat about how to tread water. He purposely waited to come to the disciples in what I believe was a test. Peter took the bait.

The incident offers a profound and teachable moment for disciples then and now, which has to do with being distracted and the consequence of distraction. It also has to do with what it means to trust. It was a lesson learned out on the water, not in a classroom.

In truth, Peter learned the lesson of trust in both his walk and his sinking failure. Peter didn't become the saint we know because he always got it right. He failed a lot, and that was the key to maturity. Jesus calls us to chew our way through, and that's the secret to maturity. Zan Holmes, retired homiletics professor from Perkins School of Theology, once said, "Jesus believed in leading his disciples in to the discovery of truth for themselves, for Jesus knows there's not much that could happen through you until it first happens to you."[81] Jesus believed in discipling his followers to the faith that would set them free (Jn 8).

---

[81] Zan Holmes, "The Lesson of the Loaves," (sermon, First United Methodist Church, Houston, May 29, 2002).

Kristopher Norris observes another important revelation about the missing missional component of the church, "I believe that for too long Protestant churches have focused on correct doctrine at the expense of right practice—orthodoxy over orthopraxy—to the detriment of Jesus's social calling in the gospel."[82]

While most church leaders would agree on the emphasis on orthodoxy over praxis, there are other legitimate reasons why the church camped out on right belief. It is easier. Incarnational ministry is costly. Engagement with our context is costly, and something will always be sacrificed when you and I incarnate like the Lord.

More about Honeybees

The honeybee begins as a tiny white egg at the bottom of a hexagon-shaped cell. It takes her twenty-one days to emerge from her hexagon. In order for her to emerge, she has to chew her way through a capping. Other bees don't help her with this. In fact, it would be an enormous waste of energy to help all these emerging bees from their cells. God engineered them to breach the barrier on their own.

This is the key to the future strength of the bee. Like any other species in nature, they must achieve life through barriers. Strength, endurance, and fortitude are acquired when we chew our way through the countless barricades of life. Whether it's the animal world or the human world, it makes no difference to God. God's process for maturing is the same across the board.

We will call the emerging baby bee a new convert to the faith. She has chewed her way to life and has joined the countless thousands of brothers and sisters. She is not fully mature yet. Actually, when baby bees are born, they look like they have been dusted with baby powder, and their wings are not fully developed. That is, they are not able to take flight when they are born. They are purposely underdeveloped so they can't leave the colony.

In the honeybee world, newborn bees stay in the colony for a few weeks. They are nursery workers. If the newborn bee's wings were fully

---

[82] Norris, *Pilgrim Practices*, Kindle location 784.

developed at birth, they more than likely would leave the colony in search of food, leaving an unattended nursery. Who would feed baby larvae, clean cells, feed the queen, and receive food from foragers? God intentionally underdeveloped the baby bees so they would stay in the nursery and care for the queen and her prodigy. A colony can't survive without a nursery!

Neither can a church survive without a nursery. Our baby converts can't endure unless they are involved in the nursery. Many of the Christians in our local congregations have a powdery look about them. Their wings are underdeveloped. They haven't been pushed and pulled through our colony. Some are still in the hexagon cells and haven't chewed their way through. The church hasn't facilitated a process of maturing baby Christians into fully developed foragers for God. They have not attended to a push-and-pull process. Collapse is inevitable unless there is a process to take our baby bees from infancy to maturity.

At one point in time, each of us has been a baby in the faith. Can you recall the people around you who discipled you? They taught you the faith and how to listen to the Spirit. They helped you understand scripture and who God really is. They taught you the disciplines that would help you flourish as a Christian. They taught you how to be self-feeders.

A beehive functions the same way. Baby bees (converts) are born and, as described previously, are pushed and pulled. They are pushed by the converts being born behind them and are pulled by the foragers ahead of them. This push and pull is essential to the survival of the hive. It is a process of maturing the residents of the colony. In this push-and-pull journey, the bees are developing and growing. They start at the center of the colony. This is where the nursery is. As their three-week nursery life continues, they are constantly being pulled to the entrance. They are moving closer and closer to their mission field.

It is important to understand this because God is about process whether in the honeybee world or human world. Every life form must breach barriers in order to reach maturity. In a beehive, bees have to chew their way to life and continue to be pushed and pulled. We call this accountability and mentorship in the church. Young Christians are not ready for the mission field. They require life-on-life relationships that can mentor them to maturity.

A large portion of our growth, however, will come through engagement with the mission field. It is believed that the apostle Paul spent nearly two years in Antioch following his conversion. In that time, faithful and mature followers of Jesus mentored him. Likewise for a period of time, Jesus mentored his disciples and made a significant investment in them. He pushed them into the mission field, and eventually they would be pulled to full-time residents of their cultural context.

The book of Acts records the maturity of the disciples and their ability to hear/sense the Spirit. They were our first semioticians, I suspect. They didn't begin as mighty apostles for Jesus Christ, but a master beekeeper fashioned them. He chiseled away at his disciples, and eventually they became fruitful promoters and disciple makers themselves. Of course, they weren't done growing and failing.

Does your church have a process of push and pull? Is there a system of accountability whereby young disciples of Jesus can become fully mature followers of Jesus? Do you have mature Christians in your church who can disciple the baby bees? I know the questions above lack a flare or flash.

In a church world where gimmicks are revered and large numeric gains rule the day, these questions may seem irrelevant. I would maintain, however, that there is nothing irrelevant about Jesus's commission to make disciples. I'm afraid attractional, gimmick-based programs, and large numeric increases aren't a fulfillment of the Great Commission. Think smaller scale. Think intentional push and pull. Disciples are forged in accountable community- and mentor-based relationships. How do we define "disciple" then, and where does this ancient process begin?

Disciple can be defined in numerous ways. Its basic meaning is "learner" or "pupil."[83] In the New Testament, the Greek word *mathētēs*, which means "disciple," is found exclusively in the gospels and the book of Acts. George Peters, in "The Call of God," defines his understanding of what a follower of Jesus is. He writes,

> A Christian disciple is more than a believer. A disciple is
> more than a learner, at least, a learner in ordinary sense of

---

[83] *Holman Illustrated Bible Dictionary*, s.v. "disciple," (Nashville: Holman Bible Publishers, 2003).

the word. A disciple is more than a follower and imitator
of Christ, more than a holy enthusiast for Christ, yea even
more than living a life of full devotion to the Lord. A
disciple is a believing person living a life of conscious and
constant identification with the Lord in life, death, and
resurrection through words, behavior, attitudes, motives,
and purpose, fully realizing Christ's absolute ownership
of his life, joyfully embracing the Saviorhood of Christ,
delighting in the Lordship of Christ and living by the
abiding, indwelling resources of Christ according to the
imprinted pattern and purpose of Christ for the chief end
of glorifying his Lord and Savior.[84]

"Although Paul never uses the term, he often describes those who
had the characteristics of being disciples."[85] Matthew uses the term
"disciple" seventy-two times in sixty-nine verses. The word "disciple"
begins to disappear from the Bible in the book of Acts, and it never
occurs in the Epistles. This reflects the transition to the "corporate
discipling" of the church. This represents a clear contrast with the one-
on-one, leader-to-follower approach of the gospels.[86]

Discipleship then is the process of apprenticing a student to follow
the living Christ. "A disciple was someone who learned a skill or way of
life from a teacher."[87] Richard Calenberg notes,

The historical roots of discipleship are found in the
terminology and practice of the Greek philosophical
schools, after which the Hebrew rabbinical schools were
patterned. Chief characteristics of discipleship included
submission to the teaching of the master teacher, a close

---

[84] George W. Peters, "The Call of God," *Bibliotheca Sacra* 120 (1963): 327.

[85] *Holman Treasury of Key Bible Words: 200 Greek and 200 Hebrew Words Defined and Explained*, s.v. "word," (Nashville: Broadman & Holman Publishers, 2000).

[86] Stuart K. Weber and Max Anders, *Holman New Testament Commentary—Matthew*, vol. 1 (Nashville: Broadman & Holman Publishers, 2000).

[87] Leonard Sweet and Frank Viola, *Jesus: A Theography* (Nashville: Thomas Nelson Publishing, 2012), 130.

personal living relationship with him, and propagation of his teaching.[88]

Calenberg also adds, "All believers were challenged to meet the demands of discipleship (submission to His authority, denial of self, service, etc.) and only who did were 'truly' disciples (John 8:31)."[89] Daniel Malone affirms, "Under Hellenistic academic influence, the Rabbinate developed fellowships of disciples and traditions of interpretation."[90]

In addition to Greek and Rabbinic schools being mentor/model-based and deeply relational, they also were noted for one more shared aspect. Calenberg observes,

> By way of observation it is further apparent that the Jewish schools reflect the same basis characteristics as the Greek school:
>
> (I)   Both were fellowships of disciples gathered around an authoritative master teacher.
>
> (II) Both were characterized by learning not only through the teaching of the master but also by observation and imitation of his life in living situations.
>
> (III) Both were committed to the important task of perpetuating the tradition associated with master and the school."[91]

One of the most impactful books on disciple making is Bill Hull's *Jesus Christ Disciplemaker*. Hull notes four distinct phases in Jesus's process of recruiting and making disciples.

---

[88] Richard D. Calenberg, "The New Testament Doctrine of Discipleship," (PhD diss., Grace Theological Seminary, 1981), 1.

[89] Ibid.

[90] Daniel Malone, "Riches and Discipleship," *Biblical Theology Bulletin* 9 (1979): 81.

[91] Calenberg, *The New Testament Doctrine of Discipleship*, 30.

First, in the case of the early disciples, he provided a four month introductory course in the ministry—*come and see*—followed by a short but meaningful opportunity to think it over. Only then did he directly challenge them—*come and follow me*. The third phase of training was *come and be with me*. The last phase of this model is *remain in me*.[92]

Jesus began relationships with the disciples before actually calling them to follow. Within this process, Jesus called and trained his disciples. Jesus formed an accountable community while living an incarnational and missional posture. The result was a movement that transformed the world. It was sustained by the fact Jesus had trained and equipped his disciples in person. The last command Jesus gave his disciples in Matthew was to multiply, in essence, to do what he had done in them.

Disciples are grounded by chewing through and living out their faith in context. If young disciples are to acquire life, they must breach barriers like nonacceptance of others for their faith, persecution, disease, death, fear, influence of addiction, disobedience, comparing self to others, education, burnout, and so on. Once barriers are breached, disciples can taste the fruit of what it means to live a full life with God. All our lives find us chewing through the obstacles that life throws at us. Those who decide not to chew their way through end up dying to the life God calls them.

If a bee can manage to chew her way through and breach the barrier, abundant life awaits her. This will not be the last wall she has to surmount. Greater barriers will be waiting for her in the fields beyond her walls. Her life thus far has prepared her to take flight. After being born and nurtured in a highly socialized world, she will spread her wings and take an orientation flight. Before leaving the colony for fields of nectar and pollen, she must grow up.

I know I left you hanging. You were probably wondering what matures this baby honeybee. What takes her from underdeveloped to fully developed forager? What will help her little wings develop? The answer to those questions lies in the field!

---

[92] Bill Hull, *Jesus Christ Disciplemaker* (Grand Rapids, MI: Baker Books, 1984), 100.

While maturing baby bees are taking care of the nursery, adult and fully mature bees are in the field, collecting resources for the colony. The babies can't grow up without the work of foragers, and foragers won't survive without nursery workers. This holy process benefits both baby and adult bee. Neither can live nor flourish without the other. Baby disciples and mature adult disciples live by the same mutual and holy benefit. Growth for either of them would be impossible without the other. The bee's governing system relies exclusively on the other. Foragers provide a necessary food for the baby bees that will advance them to maturity. Without it, a colony can't mature its young.

What is the first thing the spring of the year produces? You guessed it, pollen, the food that takes underdeveloped bees and makes them champions of the colony. What does every maturing organism need in order to survive and bear fruit?

If you answered "the sustaining power of the Holy Spirit," you would be right. However, that's not the answer I had in mind. The answer to the question is protein. Life can't exist without it. Pollen is protein. Foragers move from flower to flower, collecting protein for the nursery. Baby bees need protein to bring them to maturity. Beekeepers can feed syrup to their hearts' content, but if no protein is coming into the hive, the colony can't raise its young. Who would have guessed that pollen would be that crucial to honeybees?

The process of maturing young converts to fully devoted followers of Jesus Christ is important. The pollen we are feeding them should be equally nourishing to soul and mind. Many in the contemporary church suggest we haven't been feeding our young the deep resources of our faith. Rather we have been feeding them carbohydrates. The diets of many Christians, old and young, have been lacking the protein to help them mature. The decline and collapse of the church testifies to our methodology and diet. Growing disciples need vast amounts of protein, which is found in the fields of faith and at the feet of mature foragers.

As I see it, the modern church lacks the process of maturing our bees and is deficient in content and mission (nourishing pollen). In a pollen-less environment, maturity is stifled. Young Christians have no process for maturity, and few persons mature enough to lead them. The gimmicks, programs, and events are not a part of the process and don't offer enriching protein to sustain faith. Many Christians are biblically illiterate and have never done life with mentors. That's unfortunate. The older and more mature bees of our colony should be discipling the emerging bees and helping them to grow through life's challenges. Sadly, supposedly mature Christians have themselves been exclusively fed carbohydrates, leaving them incapable of discipling others.

Reflecting on my own process of maturing faith, I recall the friends and mentors God provided for my development and the high concentration of protein I received at their feet. Several years ago, I returned to higher education to fulfill a call to write and earn a doctorate of ministry degree. My studies led me to George Fox Evangelical Seminary. I joined the Semiotic and Future Studies Program and was placed in a cohort with fifteen others, my learning group for the next three years.

This cohort with a lead mentor provided the sustaining nourishment I desperately needed in my ministry. It was the pollen I needed to take flight in a new direction. I learned a lot about the faith. The greatest revelations were how stuck I was in my journey and how little I really knew about discipleship. In this cohort, God planted the idea of connecting discipleship with beekeeping. The connection was forged through countless hours of babbling on to my wife and thinking about how God matures life. I realized there really isn't any difference between the system God uses in creation to bring maturity and reproduction and the framework Jesus used to forge his disciples to maturity and multiplication. Multiplication is possible and probable with maturity.

The accountable community we find in honeybees, we also find in Jesus. The push and pull we find in a colony of honeybees, we find in Jesus. Graduation to the mission field from the nursery is also a component of Jesus's ministry. What Jesus taught was pollen-rich and a vital part of his methodology for maturing his followers. Pollen has come to represent both the high-protein relationships that nourish our walk with Jesus Christ and the deep content of the gospel of Jesus Christ. Pollen is the protein the body of Christ desperately needs in order to make disciples. Pollen for the hive of the church can only be found by maturing bees living incarnationally and missionally in the fields around the hive.

How's your pollen intake? Are the deep pollen relationships of incarnational living nourishing you and your church family? The fields are ready for a visit from God's pollinators. A sign of maturity of your faith community is their missional and incarnational presence in the context they are supposed to be ministering. Missional and incarnational living are two important sides of the hexagon of life. Another important side of the hexagon follows.

The True Nature

The true nature of a colony of honeybees is sacrificial. It is their credo or their mantra. Everything is done for the sake of the whole in a hive. The mission of the colony is to perpetuate their species. Each bee's entire life is completely given to the betterment of the whole. A worker honeybee will actually work herself to death. Her wings will literally fall off.

On a recent Sunday evening, I was resting in my recliner. It had been a long day, and I sent my brain on a holiday in front of the TV. On temporary sabbatical, I turned the TV station to one of my favorites, the Outdoor Channel. My favorite personality on this network is Jim Shockey and his show, *Uncharted*. On one particular episode, Jim was hunting for bears in a lush, dense forest. He and his cameraman and a couple other hunters were following the river, looking for bears. While walking up the small river, they started seeing salmon spawning. They also noticed dead salmon on the banks where the bears had been eating.

Standing by the river, Jim made two statements worthy of inclusion here, "Death begets life" and "Nothing is wasted."

The salmon come up into fresh water and lay their eggs. They exist not only to breed and lay the next generation but to feed the other animals in the ecosystem. The salmon run is a death run. The death of the salmon is the source of life to many other species up and down the river, including humans. No part of the salmon is wasted. Everything gets eaten and absorbed. The salmon is the staple for that environment, and its death begets life for others.

The honeybee, like the salmon, is a staple for our life on God's creation. Both species sacrifice their lives for future generations. Their mantra is "Death begets life." Their entire life is sacrificial. When you and I observe creation, hopefully we can see the connections God supplies and how every living thing God made is linked and purposeful. Creation tells of a God who made a system to mature the young. Life in this system is cherished and only occurs when death precedes it. "Death does beget life."

We have no greater example of this than in the life of Jesus Christ. The gospels record the God-Man sacrificially giving himself to death so all humanity may find life. Nothing about what Jesus did was wasteful. If the church is to find life, it will also have to recover the theology of death. We will have to recover the doctrine of dying to self, a painful barrier to breach but a necessary one if we are to truly live.

Any attempt to make followers of Jesus without dying to self-interest won't produce disciples. Modeling sacrificial love is the way of Jesus. It is the way God made his planet. For in it is a reminder that we are not the center of the universe. Creation whispers sacrificial discipleship.

Every time you see a bee foraging on a flower or stealing the sweet juice out of a trash can, remember the sacrifice that bee is making for the sake of her hive. Remember also she has had to chew her way to abundant life. The bee you and I see has given her life for the sake of her family's mission. Our church family mission is to make followers of Jesus. The only way to do that is to model both dying to self and living for him. I know it's a painful barrier, but it's necessary if your ministry is to produce "milk and honey" (Ex 3:8).

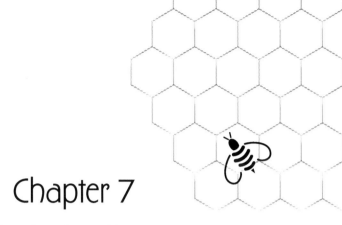

Chapter 7

Baptism from Above

Beautiful snowflakes are a baptism from above. Perhaps the most majestic and beautiful sight are towering mountains and deep gorges covered in white snow. Both beautiful and dangerous, snow-blanketed mountains fill the cornea with delight. Remember the covering of the cornea is the holy shape of a hexagon. The eyes are not the only senses that become transfixed. The smell of aspens, shrubs, and pines are equally intoxicating. Too much exposure to these elements will leave recipients in a state of introspection and tranquility, almost comatose.

Standing among giant mountains decorated in white, one is reduced to awe and praise of our Creator. One can't help but to think how awesome and imaginative God really is to have designed and sculpted those mountains. God made those beautiful mountains and trees. God is an exterior decorator. Such beautiful colors lull the observer into peace. Among those colors is one that doesn't spring naturally from the ground or the tree. The greatest color baptizes the trees and mountains from above. Dropping from above are tiny, little snowflakes. These little flakes adorn the sky and bring delight and refreshment to all.

Snowflakes freeze in the atmosphere and gently and easily float to the ground. They produce what skiers excitedly call powder. They are God's decoration and recreation but more! Life can be found from these tiny, little flakes. An accumulation of snow means life for animals, plants, fish, and humans. When the accumulated snow melts, it creates rivers of life in addition to washing and cleansing the landscape. Snowfall is baptism from above.

Baptism is our calling and our cleansing. It is the moment our identities are refreshed and realigned to Christ. Baptism is our commissioning to ministry. It is our entrance into the priesthood of all believers and ministry of Jesus Christ. Working in baptism and before is an unmerited grace.

In truth, God has been working and wooing us to acceptance before our baptism or conversion. The day we recognize and connect the dots of grace's influence on us is the day the ministry and priesthood take on a whole new significance. God is the great eye-opener to our mission to make disciples. Think for a moment about your life and story. Think about how God has connected the dots and aligned the hexagons. Consider the persons God has brought to your proximity. Consider the relationships God has opened to you. For a moment, remember the places, mentors, and divine encounters you have had. Know this: your life and mine are purposed and littered with the dots and hexagons of God's grace and connections. In those times and relationships, we were being discipled or discipling others. The mission of God was being fulfilled.

There is something refreshing or cleansing when we and the broader church live out our mission to make followers of Jesus. When the bride of Christ remembers the divine process of discipleship, we will experience a baptism from above. I can almost feel the snowflakes alighting on the church.

As noted previously, one of the life-giving sides of a hexagon is our mission. Foundational to any spiritual movement is living out our mission in the context God has given us. Loving the world is our holy mission. Pollinating the world with the love of God is undoable apart from the process of discipleship.

The mission of a hive of honeybees is to live and perpetuate their kind. Attending to the nursery is how they fulfill their mission to pollinate their context. Attending to the nursery of the church is how the church will perpetuate its kind. The church hive will have both nursery attendants and field workers. Both are needed and required to fulfill their mission to live and multiply.

Love is our mission. It is the side of the hexagon that cannot be sidestepped or reduced to mediocrity. If it is, disciples won't be made.

If it lived out in the process of forming others, then the disciples being reproduced will model that behavior for the next generation of believers. You can have every mechanical process you want to make fully committed disciples of Jesus, but if you don't model and teach love, you will be wasting your time. Love that is beautifully and sacrificially lived out is attractive and transformative. It's like a refreshing stream that gives life and renewal to whatever it touches.

Love dances, plays, and sings. Like honeybees, discipleship is a dance of love. It is the melody of the church and our lives. Love is lived out or modeled. Every attribute of love is on display for the world to see. In truth, love is more caught than taught. People are firsthand witnesses to our behavior, our generosity, our forgiveness, our gratitude, our peace, and our joy. All these attributes tell the story of our lives and the faith we profess. They speak to the indwelling or nondwelling of the Holy Spirit in your life and mine. Love above all is received and shared. The scripture tells us "that we love because he first loved us." The Bible tells us that there is nothing greater than love. God's creation speaks of a God who wonderfully and masterfully made his creation to love and care for his creation. Honeybees are a beautiful expression of that love for us.

Ultimately the greatest expression of God's love is found in the Great Honeybee we know as Jesus Christ. The giving of his life for humanity (his hive) has changed the world. Death begets life. Whether in creation or the great revelation of Jesus Christ, life can't emerge without death. Love is sacrificial. If you are living a life without a sacrificial heart, you're not living for Jesus. If love's fruit, generosity, can't be found in us, we are missing something foundational to life, love. Numerous Christians dancing together in love creates an indescribable beat. It is a remarkable sound to hear thousands of bees flapping their wings.

Christian disciples have, as Alan Hirsch once noted, "died to their own agenda." That's what it means to be Christian and to live for the lordship of Jesus Christ. Your will and way are abandoned for a higher will and way. When Jesus is Lord, we are not. The lordship of Jesus is the love relationship with Jesus. In that relationship, love and her fruit reign.

I know what you're thinking about now. You're thinking: what do snowflakes have to do with discipleship and love? And how does all of that relate to honeybees? This is a dot moment for us. It is time to connect and explain the picture you have been trying to figure out. Before I give you some dots, let me share an experience I had not too long ago.

My wife, kids, and I were on vacation in south central Colorado some time ago. We were lodging at the edge of San Luis Valley at the foothills of the Rockies. On one particular day, we decided to go sightseeing and tootle around the Silverton area. As we were driving, I noticed some beautiful and very impressive mountains. Many of them still had a blanket of snow at the peak. I fell in love with their beauty. As we continued on, I started noticing some sections that had been infected by beetles. The trees were either brown or beginning to die. Vast amounts of trees on numerous mountains were painted brown. It was a little saddening to see some of the forest dying. However, death does beget life, even for the beetles. As it turns out, beetles and forest fires happen to be necessary to purge the land. As it also turns out, the snow collection and melt are necessary means to bring life and cleansing.

The modern-day North American church is closely akin to those browning forests. Dead and dying trees litter our land. The answer to our dying forest may be a refining fire. As it turns out, maybe our dying forest is a necessary loss in order for fresh life and new discipleship to emerge. The church needs a good snowfall to help us recover our mission to love God's world. The practice of discipleship is the means to the end.

I almost forgot about the dots. You recall previously when I told you how human beings were made from the dust of the earth. Out of or from the hexagon, life emerges. The Hebrew image is God sitting at a potter's wheel, cranking the pedal with one foot and reaching to the ground with his opposite hand to grab some earth. The Divine Potter places the earth on the wheel and begins to shape man from the earth. I would like to think that, when the Potter grabbed a handful of carbon, he also grabbed a handful of snow! Why snow? You see, snow is a collection of snowflakes. Snowflakes that baptize the earth and bring life and cleansing are the holy shape of a hexagon.

The love side of a hexagon is necessary for life to emerge. The Holy Spirit baptizes us from above with power to love and be loved. He does so long before we are born again and baptized with water. You see, the artisan God who made man from the earth also made the hexagon.

That seemingly simple shape has the power to bring life whether in the beehive, a dead lion, eyeball, the earth, or snow falling down from the heavens.

The hexagon of discipleship has six necessary sides. When all sides are in operation, discipleship occurs, and we receive a new baptism from above. The dead lion of the modern church just may have something strong and sweet. God may be saying something to us from the honeycomb about death begetting life and our renewed mission to love his world. But that will never occur without being missionally focused and incarnationally present in our contexts.

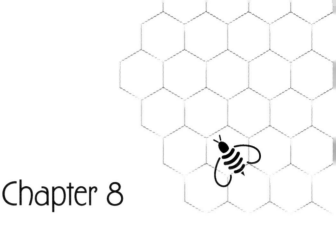

Chapter 8

The Mission of the Christian

So I have come down to rescue them from the hand of
the Egyptians and to bring them up out of that land into
a good and spacious land, a land flowing with milk and
honey—the home of the Canaanites, Hittites, Amorites,
Perizzites, Hivites and Jebusites.   —Exodus 3:8 (NIV)

Eat honey, my son, for it is good; honey from the comb
is sweet to your taste.   —Proverbs 24:13 (NIV)

I was visiting my aunt and uncle in Northern California one summer
not too many years ago. My uncle, like my father, began keeping bees
when he was a young boy. On my visit, my uncle began to tell me about
how he used to keep two queen colonies and how he merged them. He
showed me a picture of one of his beekeeper friends standing next to
this tower of deep boxes. The logic behind running two queen colonies
is you produce more honey because it takes fewer bees to maintain the
nest, which subsequently frees more foragers to gather nectar, pollen,
propolis, and water. It sounds logical if the bees have enough to forage
and a world champion seven-foot bodybuilder is on staff. It's impractical
not to mention the bees are overly aggressive in these colonies.

You might be wondering how two queens can coexist in one colony.
Basically, two hives are merged together with a combined four boxes. You
couldn't have one queen because she doesn't emit enough pheromones
for four deep boxes. A second queen is needed to both lay additional

eggs and produce enough pheromones to fill the colony. A two-queen colony has fifteen to twenty pounds of bees and can fill numerous honey supers. The question remains: how can a colony exist with two queens?

The answer is that, in normal circumstances, it doesn't. In between the four deep boxes, you put what beekeepers call an "excluder." Typically one is put on top of brood boxes to keep the queen from laying in honey supers.

The excluder between the four boxes allows all the bees except the queens and drones from passing through. Merging the two colonies together is not as simple as combining them with an excluder. There are some other procedures and techniques to use to make them successful. The queens are unable to get to each other to kill one another.

While two queen colonies can produce vast amounts of honey, they are very impractical and labor-intensive and make aggressive bees. Certain instances might be ideal for this kind of beekeeping. The idea that the nursery in a two-queen colony doesn't require as many attendants to care for the nursery, thereby freeing up foragers to collect needed resources, sounds intriguing.

The goal of many modern-day churches is to gather more bees and build and add more boxes, ministries, campuses, and so on. The dream of most aspiring pastors is to build a larger church with spectacular, sensational, and extraordinary programs and ministries. This model of ministry is very taxing on the pastors and key ministry people in the church. Leaders can literally work themselves to death to keep up the attractional gimmicks and performances. The problem, in many cases, is the nursery of the church is forsaken for bigger populations of bees.

Two-queen colonies, like larger churches, are cumbersome to manage, typically have a corporate mind-set, and have fewer nurse bees working their nurseries. The same can be said for smaller churches who are attempting to do the same. The goal in many parishes is bigger, and that is translated as successful. It's logical, right? Reach more people, add more boxes, and fulfill the Great Commission?

I'm afraid not. I'm not arguing that adding people to the kingdom of God is a bad thing. I'm arguing growth without a maturing process relegates or reduces the church to a consumeristic, competitive and seeker-sensitive entity. The true process of discipleship, in fact, has the tendency to scare many away. The rich, young ruler in Jesus's day comes to mind.

To truly become God's missional hive, the process of push and pull, in the context of accountable community, has to be a vital component of the church's ministry life. If the process of discipleship like Jesus modeled or modeled in his creation is absent, then we will not fulfill Matthew 28.

Orientation Flight

I can imagine, when the Lord pushed his disciples in Luke 9–10 to go into villages and towns, they were uneasy with that. In fact, they were probably pretty scared. This is what we call in beekeeping the "orientation flight." As you remember, honeybees aren't born within a colony and immediately leave. They are attendants first and then later take flight.

When the disciples were first called, they were by no means ready to take flight. They observed Jesus as he modeled kingship and incarnated himself within his context. Jesus instructed them to take nothing with them. No provisions. He wanted his disciples to trust him. Jesus knew they would learn a lot. Such an experience would help them in their future ministries. There is nothing compared to getting pushed into a briar patch barefooted, as my old mentor Lee Lamb used to say.

The disciples were put out in the neighborhood. Jesus told them they would be "lambs in the midst of wolves." Don't you imagine it was a little nerve-wracking to be propelled out into neighborhoods to share the good news and have power and authority to do many miraculous things? I would be nervous! The point is what Jesus did was to prepare the disciples for future ministry and witness. The sending out of the twelve and seventy was a training exercise, and it was important that Jesus not be with them.

Many of you realize the length of time and investment that forming disciples takes. It is not just as simple as leading someone to Jesus through a prayer or even modeling right behavior and discipline before him or her. This process of taking an apprentice is lengthy and involves a lot of heart. There will come a time though when the persons you are helping to form in the faith will need to take their orientation flight. They can no longer stay within the safety of your presence. As you push on them, God is pulling them to incarnational ministry. The ultimate goal is for your disciples to become self-feeders and multiply Christ in others! The model you set for them will more than likely be the model they share with their disciples.

The sending out is our mission. To be incarnational is to be present within the community you live in. To be a disciple of Jesus is to be in mission to make more disciples of Jesus out in the neighborhood.

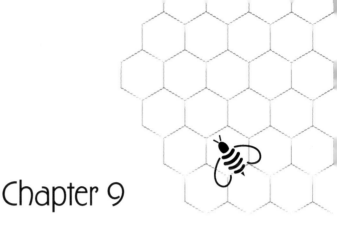

Chapter 9

The Lion and the Honeybees

I never imagined this book would become what it has. The beauty of choosing a novel metaphor to unpack the greatest practice in history has created a blessed union. What was unleashed is a wealth of symbolism, uncanny connections, and sacredness that was lost to our remembered past.

When I started this project, I simply wanted to bolster the practice of discipleship in the local church. What I didn't know or could have never imagined is beekeeping would be married to discipleship and give us something sweet for the future of the church. The one question I asked myself about Samson's riddle is why a swarm of bees would make their home in the carcass of a lion. I understand the story symbolically. However, the more I thought about the bees in the lion, the more I realized the riddle has untold and numerous lessons for life and, of course, discipleship.

Beyond the symbolic is the literal. Journey with me for a moment for a literal rendering of the text. If you think about it, the lion carcass makes a perfect home for a swarm of bees. Several scout bees would have investigated the remains, invited others to take a look, and then made a collective decision to move to the dead lion. The secret to a hive swarming into a lion is not because it makes a wonderfully symbolic story, though it does. The secret is not that the bees collectively made a decision and swarmed in to the carcass. The secret lies in the question, "Why would they?" The secret to their location choice is the indestructible and insulated hide of the lion. The only reason a swarm would make its hive in a carcass of a lion is if it made a good home. This means they would be able to regulate the temperature. Regulated temperature translates into raising their young. The bees wouldn't have picked a lion carcass unless it was a suitable home to raise and mature their offspring. A beekeeper would have asked the question of home selection but also would know the answer to the question pretty readily. The answer is a good home.

It is easy to be deconstructive and critical in our analysis of the modern church. To be sure, there are enormous deficits and monumental failures we have to come to terms with. However, being overly critical and not offering solutions to the problems we face is shortsighted. For all its failures, there is something strong and sweet we can digest. For emerging out of the dead lion are some renewed theologies and practices and imaginative solutions for our current state. Deficits do create abundances on the other end of the spectrum. Declines, deficits, and failures are catalytic in their ability to deepen and extend us in ways we never imagined. The decline of the church and its failure to make deeply committed followers of Jesus may prove fertile soil for future disciple making. What may emerge from the soil is a more authentic expression of Christian faith and practice. We may also discover some of our biblical and theological lenses have been inadequate to deal with cultural shifts. Decline bolsters revelation, and God is reimagined. The mystery of our faith resurfaces.

This makes many uneasy. There are questions of how we interpret the Bible, who our neighbor is, and what God is saying in the midst of a very noisy culture and disoriented lion. There is good in the lion in spite of it wobbling around in a daze. God still uses the church and calls people from the body.

The church that raised me to maturity and affirmed my call helped me envision a new community. I found discipline and love there. The church is my home, and they have regulated and provided a place for me to flourish in the ministry. They have been my lion's hide covering and hexagon of discipleship.

The hope that the dead lion will be resurrected is yet to be decided. There is some measure of hope in this writer about the future of the church. The church, however, will more than likely be much different from the current reality. It will be so only because the culture of discipleship will have planted itself in the cavity of the dead lion. The lion will never be the same. What has swarmed into her and vicariously and incarnationally lives out of the lion are the sacred honeybees.

An important quality a disciple of Jesus needs is courage to follow even if the circumstance or situation warrants fear. The apostle Peter stepping out of the boat, the disciples surrendering to the call of the Master, and the disciples being sent out into the mission field two by two are examples of needed trust and courage. That sort of trust and courage was no doubt modeled by Jesus when he walked on water, surrendered to his divine call, lived incarnationally in his mission field, and, on numerous occasions, excused himself from the crowd to spend time with the Father.

There are many in the modern church who have and many more who will step a little closer to the divine call to tell a discipleship narrative. Obtaining the sweet surprise from the lion calls for courage. It actually takes real courage to close the gap between you and the beehive. Courage to venture close to the hive is only accompanied by the tools necessary for robbing the sweet honey from the lion. Discipleship is risky, and the possibility of being stung is high. However, the reward for creating a discipleship culture and venturing close to that lion is the sweetest reward of life. The good news is we don't have to journey toward the lion without tools.

A beekeeper never enters the beehive without two tools: a smoker and a hive tool to pry the lid and boxes apart. Approaching a hive without these tools would be the equivalent of petting a wild bear. You just don't do it. Courage is needed as much as the tools to get the job done. Can you, in your ministry context, approach the lion and his bees? Not without others to help you learn and some experience under your belt. Telling and living a cultural narrative of disciple making will no doubt stir the colony to excitement and anger. You will get stung in your pursuit to help the church make followers of Jesus. Courage to keep moving toward the beehive is absolutely necessary.

Let me *bee* very clear with you. Honeybees have to be investigated, worked, and fed. It takes real faith and courage to lift the lid of a beehive and an aggressive church. When a beekeeper works bees, he or she will more than likely get stung. It's a part of the vocation. Pastors and professional ministry people will get stung when they attempt to correct the ills of the church.

Before spring emerges and flowers begin to bloom, most astute apiarists will begin feeding their bees in January. They will feed syrup (carbohydrate) and pollen patties (protein). Feeding encourages the queen to begin laying. However, when lifting the lid in early January to feed, beekeepers find more aggressive bees. It is, however, worth a few stings to encourage colonies to growth. When you and I begin to plant the culture of discipleship in a church and retell the narrative, expect angry bees when you lift the lid and begin to pour on the food. They will despise you early on but praise you later.

Many years ago, I went to work for my grandfather in his commercial beekeeping operation. I remember my first time to suit up. All the proper clothes and head coverings were put on, and the smoker was ignited. The first lesson my grandfather taught me was not to block the entrance of the beehive with my body. I had knelt down in front of the entrance and disturbed the flight path of the bees. Grandpa told me to move around to the side. Easy enough.

I gave the hive several puffs from the smoker to calm the bees and learned my second lesson when he said, "That's enough." I was putting too much smoke on the hive. He pried off the lid, smoked it, and commenced to moving and pulling frames, starting from the outside and working his way to the middle. Sitting with him, I watched what he did, how he did it, and how quickly/slowly he did it. His eyes were seeing things that would take me years to finally observe. I remember being intimidated by the thousands of bees flying all around me and being amazed at how my grandfather seamlessly negotiated all the colonies we checked that day.

The hive buried in the lion of the church has something sweet for us. It will take courage, tools, and even experienced people to help us negotiate those hives. Make no mistake. Every beekeeper will be stung thousands of times over his or her life. Sometimes it doesn't matter how much smoke you pour over a hive. They are still extremely agitated by your presence and the disruption that discipleship makes. Even the most experienced practitioners of disciple making will be stung, no matter how much sensitivity is applied. If there is anything that will stir up a church, it is attempting to change the culture they have grown accustomed to. Moving the church from institution where gimmicks, events, programs, and Bible study are the bread and butter of their cultural life is challenging. What is missing from their community is a robust discipleship. What is missing is the honey for their bread and butter. The honeybees are a gift from the Creator, and it will summon our best courage to discover the sweetness that lies just beneath the lid.

God designed honeybees to make disciples and created them to be missional, community-oriented, and incarnational. The bees can't survive and flourish without each of these. Honeybee colonies hold the secret to disciple making. God gave them to us to teach us. What we learn is that, the same process of push and pull we find in Jesus's ministry, we find in a colony of honeybees.

The Samson riddle is about the future. It is a declaration of the future of God's chosen people. The lion represents a lost and dead people. The hope of the riddle is what has taken up residence in the dead lion. It satisfies the eyes, nose, and ears. It offers new hope and life through a hexagon. It is dripping with honey. It is discipleship. You see, the future hope of Israel, the modern church, and our homes lie with rediscovering the sacred bee of Jesus Christ and the process he created to bring life and maturity to his creation.

Buried within scripture is the powerful metaphor of beekeeping. Whoever could have imagined that deep within the scriptures we would discover one of the most profound examples or metaphors of what it means to follow Jesus Christ (our Great Honeybee). The scripture and creation has revealed the sacred honeybee of Jesus Christ and the holy process of discipleship he gave us. We need only find that holy process in the life of Jesus and underneath the lid of his beehive. What is needed is courage and tools to open up the lion and rediscover the hexagon of discipleship. There we will find the most amazing source of life. We will see, taste, hear, touch, and smell the goodness of the Lord and a church flowing with honey from the hexagon.

The mission of the Christian and church is to make followers of Jesus Christ. The mission is fulfilled when the church is reengaged in missional/incarnational ministry, accountable community, education, mentorship, sacrifice, and clustering. Life and discipleship is reawakened when these six become paramount in a church body. Pastors and ministry leaders and teams can and should be living and speaking this language. However, many times the pool for mature disciples can be shallow. Unless the church is living these components of discipleship, they will never multiply the way the Lord is calling them to. Very briefly let me recap the sides of the hexagon.

The Hexagon

The missional/incarnational life is one where we live in the communities God plants us. Our ministry and reach is largely in the community. Our mission is to make followers of Jesus by first getting to know the people/families of our community. This is what it means to live incarnationally. While we live incarnationally, we never lose the mission that our responsibility is to help those we are meeting come to follow Jesus.

While we are expanding our incarnational reach, we do so in the context of accountable community. We gather strength, encouragement, building-up, and love from the people of the church or covenant community we are a part of. The church needs us, and we need them. We need the other bees in the colony to help push and pull us to deeper faith and mission.

This community of faith is also responsible for educating us in the biblical story and all its varied lessons and truths. The education we receive from disciple makers is not just to make sure we are biblically fluent. The community of faith teaches us how to worship, pray, and understand the magnificence of God and subtleties and nuances of the Holy Spirit. They help us to "chew our way through." The community of faith serves its function but cannot replace the next side of the hexagon.

Buried within the community of faith are mentors who model life and faith. They are the joyful people who surround us. They are the encouragers who pour into our souls. They are the mothers and fathers of our faith. They are the ones who pick us out of the crowd and invite us to deeper fellowship and accountability. Mentors push on us and pull us. They are the ones who get the gospel, live and love the gospel, and model gospel living. Experienced practitioners of the faith and Spirit listeners are words we use to describe them. This group is in short supply in most contexts. They model, and their followers imitate their walk.

Mentorship done correctly bears the mark of the X. Creating self-feeding, maturing, and obedient followers of Jesus Christ is our mission. The true sign that a person is proficient at making followers is if their disciples multiply. Jesus made disciples who made more followers. The DNA of these disciples was sacrifice. Disciples who don't commit their lives to the Lord and die to their own agenda don't replicate the model of Jesus.

The hexagon above is creative. The six sides are important components to transforming lives. Pushing and pulling willing participants to faith and maturity is our calling. It seems clear that the operative word is "willing." How many ministry settings have you been in where you tried to push and pull the unwilling to deeper faith and commitment? I can answer numerous. You and I can't take people where they are unwilling to go. What aids disciple makers in creating a discipleship culture fulfills the six sides and actually makes followers the last side. This last side will be discussed in the final chapter.

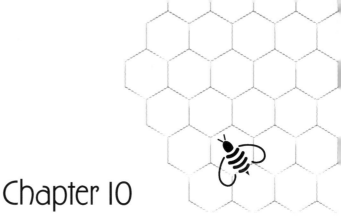

Chapter 10

Clustering and Conclusion

A s a beekeeper and pastor, I have made nearly every mistake you can make in trying to do what God has asked of me. I have failed on every front but learned some valuable lessons through the "sacrament of failure."[93] I have had to chew my way through some difficult lessons.

One such lesson in beekeeping is tending to the cluster. There was a time in my early beekeeping where I didn't understand my role as beekeeper was one of stewardship. I told myself the bees would make up the honey I had taken from them and protect themselves from pests and disease without my help. I somehow thought that only the strong would survive. Poor management on my part translated to weak or dead colonies. What I didn't know is that every spring I should be preparing for next spring in my management of the bees.

Ministry is really no different. You're always preparing for future ministry and discipleship. If you're not, then you won't be doing much of either. Likewise, I have both failed and succeeded in the ministry. One lesson learned is ministry isn't mechanics. We can't just take the bullet points from someone else's presentation and duplicate them in our own. Jesus doesn't work on the safe and linear or mechanistic line of the heavily influenced leadership culture church. Ministry is journey and process. Ministry is living in the sacrament of failure with hope. Ministry truly happens in deep, abiding relationship with God and

---

[93] A phrase I picked up in conversation with Leonard Sweet at his home in Washington State, March 2015.

his people. What emerges from the hexagon and beehive is a fully committed disciple of Jesus who has the depth and experience to make more mature followers. What emerges are pollinators. If the nursery is attended, foragers will emerge. If foraging is fruitful, the nursery will flourish.

I suspect a confession is in order for our sacrament to bring life to us and conclusion to this book. Four years ago, I thought I knew something about discipleship but realized how poorly trained and proficient I was at making followers. My experience in the churches I served largely skewed my perspective of discipleship. Discipleship meant making more converts, putting them in Bible studies, and plugging them into committees. I thought this would be the winning formula. More people in the pews and increased money in the bank meant I had been successful.

Once I was awakened from my skewed perspective on discipleship, I thought I could take components from others and duplicate them in my ministry. In a very methodical and mechanical way, I tried to replicate what I had learned in my local congregation. I had even actually considered my audience to some degree. I also naïvely believed, if you changed the language of the church, you could actually change the church over time.

I spent numerous hours making this connection between beekeeping and discipleship. I struggled with the sides of the hexagon and what actually needed to be included in what is before you. However, in spite of my best ideas, language change, charisma, and knowledge of disciple making, something was missing. The bees still needed to teach something about disciple making and fruitfulness. There was something about how Jesus made followers that had eluded me in the transformation of my own disciples and context. Let's look at the honeybees and Jesus again for the something strong and sweet.

Of the many lessons we could extract from bee culture, one rises to the top for this author. And that lesson is clustering. You recall me mentioning that beekeepers are always preparing their bees for the next season. This includes treatments for bee health, food for wintering, and the work to ensure the hive is queen right and she is a good one. Going into winter with an inferior queen will create problems in your new-year buildup. As is the case for most species, it's not always about genetics.

However, good genetics play an enormous role in your colony's health and fruitfulness.

The summertime gives you a good chance to observe the laying pattern of the queen. If she isn't a strong layer, I will find her, pinch off her head, and replace her with a better queen. The ideal situation is to go in to winter with a strong colony with plenty of food reserves.

In the winter months, the bees cluster in a ball around the honey stores they have collected. There aren't any outside sources available during the winter months. They have to rely solely on what they have collected and what we have provided for them. If honey is pulled off them and not replaced with syrup, the bees will starve to death during the winter months. The queen will shut down her laying when food stops coming in the hive. If she doesn't stop laying, then there will be more bees and not enough food to feed them.

Clustering is an important time in a colony. The bees huddle together for warmth by locking their legs together. They huddle around food and the little portion of brood that remains. It is their clustering time. They depend on one another in many ways, especially for warmth. Ideally, you want to go into winter with a sizable cluster and enough food to feed them over a few months of cold.

The lesson that had eluded me in the process of attempting to change the culture of the church with a new discipleship language was clustering. The process of discipleship found in beekeeping and the template is absolutely right. There is no flaw in the process or our attempt to replicate it in our context or church. The flaw lies in us not understanding or neglecting the side of the hexagon that really matters.

I believe in seasons of our Christian life. We have time, like bees, when we proliferate and are extraordinarily fruitful in our ministry. At other times, not so much. The most fruitful and incarnational/missional churches are those who are great at discipleship because they practice clustering. What clustering does for bees, prayer does for followers of Jesus. Clustering around the nest and rich reserves of the gospel with a very intentional and committed prayer life is the warmth the church needs to make followers. When we lock arms and legs and pray together, through our differences, we are warmed beyond measure. Not only do we survive, at the center of our cluster, disciples are born and nourished by the reserves we have collected. Young and/or impressionable followers are watchful and will learn how to be disciples by our modeling behavior and practices. Disciples who are born and raised in clusters will eventually model clustering with their own disciples and churches. Disciple makers who model gimmicks, attractional ministry, and the importance of numeric growth and then neglect to teach their pupils about clustering have stolen the power out of their disciples' future ministry. Whatever bad or nonexistent habits, inconsistencies, poor theology, and poor Christian traits we have will be passed on to those we mentor in the faith. This is exactly why a high level of accountable community is important. All the deficiencies we have, in theory, should get worked out in community.

A well-laid-out plan for discipleship is ineffective unless it finds seasons of deep cluster where unity is achieved and love creates sincere warmth among the body. Jesus said his house would be a house of prayer. There is a reason why he said that and why he practiced deep and abiding relationship with the Father. It was the source of his power and strength. John 15 speaks about the branches abiding in the vine, and without the vine, the branches wither up and die. The branches cluster around the vine for life. The vine generates the nutrition and resources the branches need to produce fruit. It's the same idea as the bees but a different metaphor.

At the beginning of January, beekeepers begin to feed their bees pollen patties and syrup to jump-start the queen to laying. Patties and syrup are continued until the colony starts bringing in its own pollen. Honeybees expand rapidly and, by March, are in really good shape for the nectar flow. When temperature reaches about sixty degrees, the cluster will break and begin heading out.

Much like bees, a strong church only becomes so because it has learned how to cluster effectively. Meaningful prayer services, covenant groups, and prayer teams bless a congregation and warm them in ways no one or nothing else can. Strong disciples are built in such seasons and in strong clusters. The most important side of the hexagon is clustering, for in it we find our future without seeing it. God is revealed in fresh ways and expressions when prayer takes root in a body of believers. Courage of conviction and clarity of thought are discovered in the ball of church members clustered together to love and worship God in prayer. Clustering early in your ministry for future ministry and discipleship potential is wise advice. If you and I attempt to replicate the above sides without seeking the throne of God, often it will find us exhausted and defeated.

The hexagon produces life (honey/disciples) when the other bees in the colony attend to it. Prayer raises the production temperature of the colony. The mission of the Christian is to make followers on our knees before the Father. On our knees is where the hexagon comes together and discipleship takes root in the body of Christ.

At times and in seasons, there are more pronounced times of clustering within bee life. With sixty-thousand-plus bees in a colony, however, there is always some degree of clustering happening. Bees can get very congested and often hang out of the hive in a wall of cluster.

As you know, Jesus practiced a deep prayer life. The gospels record him pulling away from the crowds to enter into times of communion with the Father. The hallmark of Jesus's ministry was his communion with the Father. Jesus lived and walked in constant connection, uninhibited by sin and brokenness. The dependency and oneness Jesus lived with the Father was the source of power for his ministry. Jesus, no doubt, was the greatest disciple maker who ever lived. He took a band of seemingly nobody's and began a movement which regenerated the world and still transforms lives today.

As a modern follower of Jesus, the practice of clustering will be as ever vital today as it was in the first century or in a hive of honeybees. Deeply cultured prayer communities make disciples. Faith communities who spend the majority of their time entertaining and servicing their clients, promoting their theological and ecclesial brands, and using gimmicky practices don't make time for the deep and abiding prayer that will change their church culture from seeker-sensitive to a transformative body.

Someone once asked me when I moved to a new church what my plan was. I didn't have a plan other than getting to know the congregation and establishing myself in the community. The person who asked was a representative from the leadership culture. Modern church leaders, lay and clergy, are deeply invested in the leadership culture of North America.

The leadership culture has its own language and set of objectives. One of which is to make more leaders. It is efficient at promoting that agenda and multiplying results. The church has baptized the language and values of that culture and called those values Christian. The language and objectives of the church are very different. Community is exalted, family and values are promoted, and forgiveness and mercy are lived out gregariously. Love and all it signifies is championed in the community of faith. At the heart of all our ideals, beliefs, and practices is prayer. It is the glue that holds our community together. Blessed are the churches who cluster.

So many have said to me over the years, "The church is a business," "What's your plan?" or "What's our strategy?" Wrong comments and questions. In twenty years of church life, I have had only one congregation that championed prayer. It isn't any wonder why we are in decline. We not only lost the practice of discipleship but the power behind it.

If we are to become discipling churches and powerful advocates for the kingdom of God, the culture of prayer has to take center stage. When it does, we might see a new Pentecost and a deeper unity and peace among the churches. Rallying the church to prayer may be more difficult than we expect. It will take real faith and courage to branch out and step in the direction of prayer.

Is there hope for the modern church to rebound with the willing and become a disciple-making body? That depends on if the church is committed to return to clustering. Inside the dead and dying lion is the future of the church, for the bees who live there will eventually outgrow the lion and swarm out to new places and ministry contexts. Our future of discipleship will be largely dependent on our willingness to lock arms and pray together.

There is something sacred about honeybees. They are a great metaphor for understanding the process of discipleship. Like the prophet Deborah, God can still speak to us through honeybees. Samson's lion holds the future for the church, and it is strong and sweet. At the center of the lion are bees clustered around the hexagon of discipleship. New life and hope are found there in clustering posture.

The Christian faith of the twenty-first century will require awesome amounts of courage and ability to hope and see future potential out of something that is dying. The church is collapsing, but the breakdown may not be a bad thing if it means a new start. There is hope in the lion and a sweet surprise. The church as we know it is collapsing on itself. However, the church that is emerging is being formed by the hexagon of discipleship. Mike Breen, founder of 3DM, has said many times, "If you get the church, you will not always get disciples. If you get disciples you will always get the church." Truer words were never spoken.

When honeybees are clustered together in community, they make a unique buzzing sound. It is a sweet sound! It is a scary sound! When our churches learn how to cluster, we will create a very distinct BUZZ the world will hear. Clustering in prayer will provide the answer to the riddle of what is strong and sweet or how the church can flourish. What has emerged from the cluster in Samson's lion is the future of God's church, discipleship! Let's dance!

Bibliography

Amateur Entomologists Society. "Kleptoparasite." Accessed October 1, 2014. http://www.amentsoc.org/insects/glossary/terms/kleptoparasite.

Barna, George. *The State of the Church 2002.* Ventura, CA: Issachar Resources, 2002.

Beck, Bodog F., *Honey and Health: a Nutrimental, Medicinal and Historical Commentary.* New York: R. M. McBride and Co., 1958.

Breeze, Tom D., Bernard E. Vaissière, Riccardo Bommarco, Theodora Petanidou, Nicos Seraphides, Lajos Kozák, Jeroen Scheper, Jacobus C. Biesmeijer, David Kleijn, Steen Gyldenkærne, Marco Moretti, Andrea Holzschuh, Ingolf Steffan-Dewenter, Jane C Stout, Meelis Pärtel, Martin Zobel, and Simon G.Potts. "Agricultural Policies Exacerbate Honeybee Pollination Service Supply-Demand Mismatches Across Europe." *PLoS ONE,* 2014.

Cole, Neil. *Primal Fire: Reigniting the Church with the Five Gifts of Jesus.* Bonita Springs, FL: Tyndale House Publishers, 2014.

Delaney, Deborah A. "Genetic Characterization of U.S Honey Bee Populations." PhD diss., Washington State University, 2008. Accessed August 5, 2014. www.dissertations.wsu.edu/Dissertations/.../d_delaney_070108.pdf.

Feinberg, Margaret. *Scouting the Divine: my search for God in wine, wool, and wild honey.* United States: Zondervan, 2009.

Fife, Austin. "The Concept of the Sacredness of Bees, Honey and Wax in Christian Popular Tradition." PhD diss., Stanford University, 1939.

———. "Christian Swarm Charms from the Ninth to the Nineteenth Centuries," *The Journal of American Folklore* 77, no. 304 (1964): 154–159. Accessed August 2014. http://www.jstor.org/stable/537564.

Forlong, James George Roche. *Faith of Men: A Cyclopedia of Religions.* London, 1906.

Gordon, Charles R. *In Plain Sight: Seeing God's Signature throughout Creation.* Tyler, TX: 2009.

Hirsch, Alan, and Tim Catchim. *The Permanent Revolution: Apostolic Imagination and Practice for the 21st Century.* San Francisco: Jossey Bass, 2012.

Holbert, John. "Moses." Bible study at the Texas Annual Conference of the UMC, Woodlands, TX, May 2009.

Holmes, Zan. "The Lesson of the Loaves." Sermon at the Ordination Service of the Texas Annual Conference, Houston, May 29, 2002.

Hull, Bill. *The Disciple-Making Church: Leading a Body of Believers on the Journey of Faith.* Grand Rapids, MI: Baker Books, 2010.

Idleman, Kyle. *Not a Fan: Becoming a Completely Committed Follower of Jesus.* Grand Rapids, MI: Zondervan, 2011.

Johnson, Brian. "Division of Labor in Honeybees: Form, Function and Proximate Mechanism." *Behav Ecol Sociobiol* 64, no. 3 (2010): 305–316. Accessed October 2014. doi:10.1007/s00265-009-0874-7.

Jones, Brett. *Apiculture and Beekeeping Simplified.* Salt Lake City: Alpha One Publishing, 2012.

Kellogg, Vernon. *Nuova or The New Bee: A Story of Children of Five to Fifty.* Boston and New York: Houghton Mifflin Company, 1920.

McNeal, Reggie. *The Present Future: Six Tough Questions for the Church.* San Francisco: Jossey-Bass, 2003.

Moore, Lisa Jean, and Mary Kosut. *Buzz: Urban Beekeeping and the Power of the Bee.* New York: New York University Press, 2013.

Morgan, Teresa. *Literate Education in the Hellenistic and Roman Worlds.* Cambridge: Cambridge University Press, 1998.

Norris, Kristopher. *Pilgrim Practices: Discipleship for a Missional Church.* Eugene, OR: Cascade Books, 2012.

O'Malley, Michael. *The Wisdom of Bees: What the Hive Can Teach Business About Leadership, Efficiency, and Growth.* New York: Penguin Group, 2010.

Patrons of the Faith. "Patrons of Bees." Saints.SQPN.com. Last modified September 12, 2013. Accessed September 2014. http://saints.sqpn.com/patrons-of-bees.

Quinby, Moses. *Mysteries of Bee-Keeping Explained*. New York: C. M. Saxton, Agriculture Book Publisher, 1853.

Ransome, Hilda M. *The Sacred Bee in Ancient Times and Folklore*. Boston and New York: Houghton Mifflin Company, 1937.

Seeley, Thomas D. *Honeybee Democracy*. Princeton, NJ: Princeton University Press, 2010.

———. *The Five Habits of Highly Effective Honeybees: And What We Can Learn From Them*. Princeton, NJ: Princeton University Press, 2010.

Sister M. Theressa of the Cross Springer. "Nature-Imagery in the Works of Saint Ambrose." PhD diss., Catholic University of America, 1931.

Taylor, Barbara Brown. *An Altar in the World: A Geography of Faith*. New York: HarperCollins, 2009.

vanEngelsdorp, Dennis Evans JD, Claude Saegerman, Chris Mullin, Eric Haubruge, Bach Kim Nguyen, Maryann Frazier, Jim Frazier, Diana Cox-Foster, Yanping Chen, Robyn Underwood, David R. Tarpy, and Jeffrey S. Petis. "Colony Collapse Disorder: A Descriptive Study," *PLOS ONE* 4, no 8: e6481 (2009). Accessed January 1, 2014. doi:10.1371/journal.pone.0006481.

Zahnd, Brian. *Beauty Will Save The World: Rediscovering The Allure & Mystery of Christianity*. Lake Mary, FL: Charisma House Book Group, 2012.

Zucker, Lois Miles. S. "Ambrosii: De Tobia: A Commentary, with an Introduction and Translation." PhD diss., Catholic University of America, 1933.

Manufactured by Amazon.ca
Bolton, ON